200
BARBECUE RECIPES

W9-AHG-302

HAMLYN **ALL COLOR COOKBOOK**

200
BARBECUE
RECIPES

LOUISE PICKFORD

An Hachette UK company
www.hachette.co.uk

First published in Great Britain in 2009 by Hamlyn,
a division of Octopus Publishing Group Ltd,
Carmelite House, 50 Victoria Embankment,
London EC4Y 0DZ
www.octopusbooks.co.uk
www.octopusbooksusa.com

This edition published in 2016

Copyright © Octopus Publishing Group Ltd 2009, 2016

Some of the recipes in this book have previously appeared in
other books published by Hamlyn

Distributed in the US by Hachette Book Group,
1290 Avenue of the Americas, 4th and 5th Floors,
New York, NY 10020

Distributed in Canada by Canadian Manda Group,
664 Annette St., Toronto, Ontario, Canada M6S 2C8

All rights reserved. No part of this work may be reproduced or
utilized in any form or by any means, electronic or mechanical,
including photocopying, recording or by any information storage
and retrieval system, without the prior written permission of
the publisher.

ISBN 978-0-600-63357-0

Printed and bound in China

10 9 8 7 6 5 4 3 2 1

Standard level kitchen cup and spoon measurements are used
in all recipes.

Ovens should be preheated to the specific temperature; if using
a convection oven, follow manufacturer's instructions for
adjusting the time and the temperature.

Eggs should be large unless otherwise stated. The U.S. Food
and Drug Administration advises that eggs should not be
consumed raw. This book contains dishes made with raw or
lightly cooked eggs. It is prudent for more vulnerable people,
such as pregnant and nursing mothers, people with weakened
immune systems, the elderly, babies, and young children, to
avoid uncooked or lightly cooked dishes made with eggs.
Once prepared, these dishes should be kept refrigerated and
used promptly.

This book includes dishes made with nuts and nut derivatives.
It is advisable for customers with known allergic reactions to
nuts and nut derivatives and those who may be potentially
vulnerable to these allergies, such as pregnant and nursing
mothers, people with weakened immune systems, the elderly,
babies, and children, to avoid dishes made with nuts and nut
oils. It is also prudent to check the labels of prepared
ingredients for the possible inclusion of nut derivatives.

contents

introduction

introduction

The great thing about barbecues is they represent summer, and cooking and eating outdoors is about as good as it gets. Light evenings, warm weather, and the aroma of meat caramelizing over hot coals or a gas barbecue is pure bliss and is perhaps why this age-old method of cooking has evolved from the simple need to eat to the pleasurable social occasion it is today.

Although sources differ as to its origin, it is more or less recognized that the word "barbecue" comes from the Spanish word *barbacoa*, which literally means a wooden framework used to smoke meat or fish, or as a framework to sleep in!

By the eighteenth century, however, it was used to describe a means of roasting food over heat around which an entertainment event took place, and it was the Taino peoples of the Caribbean and Florida who then used the term "Taino Barbecu" or "sacred pit of fire."

From here, this method of cooking traveled throughout the American Deep South during the days of slavery, where barbecues became an important part of the social gatherings of the day. It is likely that during this period pork would have been the most common food cooked at a barbecue, as pigs were cheap. In fact, today in the US pork is still the most commonly barbecued meat.

Americans have adopted barbecuing as an important part of their culture, from barbecued ribs and steaks to the many types of fast-food joints selling burgers and the like.

Barbecuing is an excuse to get outdoors, where food seems to taste better. The food tends to be more casual and the occasion more relaxed. I think that for many of us, barbecuing has become one of our preferred methods of cooking as well as an enjoyable way of entertaining. It is a great way to cook, not only for the flavor of the food but because it's done outdoors, where we are more relaxed, informal and often happier.

types of barbecue

There are two main types of barbecue in common use and these are charcoal (or wood) and gas. They all have their advantages and disadvantages, but what they all do is cook food on a rack or grill set above the heat source. Generally, we use a barbecue to cook food over a high heat for a short amount of time, but they can also be used to great effect to slow-cook meat, often with the addition of wood chips to give a wonderful smoky flavor. I have included several recipes where you will require a barbecue with a lid, so the method becomes similar to using a conventional oven. However, the majority of the recipes can be cooked in the normal way on either a gas or charcoal barbecue.

Which is best: charcoal or gas? For flavor, I would always choose a charcoal barbecue (wood can also be used), but for convenience I have to say gas wins hands down, especially if you are only cooking for two.

charcoal barbecues

These are designed to burn coal or wood. Food cooked over coals or wood has that distinctive smoky, caramelized flavor we love so much—the outside of the food is sticky and chargrilled while the inside remains moist and succulent. However, they are messy, take longer to preheat and need constant attention.

For price and convenience, disposable charcoal barbecue sets available from many supermarkets are ideal for dinner for two.

There are also several small portable barbecues available from hardware stores and specialty suppliers, which are ideal for picnics. They are usually vented to help increase or decrease the heat, or have a rung system above the coals so the grill rack can be raised or lowered as necessary.

The "table" barbecue is basically a box on legs—the coals sit on a grate in the box with the grill rack for cooking on top of that. The rack can be raised higher or lower depending on the heat required. These often have lids.

The kettle barbecue is particularly versatile, as its shape allows the coals to sit on a grate in the drum, protected from drafts. The cooking rack sits on top and then a large dome-shaped lid can be used as a cover, transforming it into an oven. There is also a vent system that makes it easier to control the temperature.

fuels

Charcoal briquettes are the most common fuel and these are readily available from many supermarkets and hardware stores. Always read package labels, as some briquettes can contain chemicals. Hardwood lump charcoal, which contains no additives, burns easily, heats up quickly and lasts well, is harder to find, but try specialty barbecue suppliers. If burning wood, only use hardwoods such as hickory, mesquite, or oak. Apple and olive wood are also good. Wood chips are smaller chips of the same wood but these are used to create extra smoke for flavor.

lighting charcoal

Arrange a good layer of charcoal about 4 inches deep in the middle of the grate, adding in a few firelighters. Light the firelighters using matches or a taper, and leave the coals for about 40-45 minutes until they are glowing red and covered in a light gray ash.

Using a poker, garden rake, or long-handled tongs, rake the coals over the grate's surface. If you need more than one temperature, rake some of the coals on top of each other so you have an area that has a double layer. This will be the hottest area, while the single layer has a more medium heat. This should remain hot for about 1 hour, but you can add a few more coals from time to time if necessary. The barbecue is considered hot when you can hold your hand about 5 inches above the coals for just a couple of seconds, medium-hot when you can manage 3–4 seconds, and cool for 5–6 seconds. Alternatively, raise or lower the grill to alter the heat level.

lighting wood

Place a few small, dry twigs in the grate with a few firelighters. Add a good heap of wood chunks, light the firelighters and leave the wood to burn until it is glowing and ashen and no flames remain.

gas barbecues

A gas barbecue is highly practical as it can be lit in seconds and the temperature set with the twist of a knob. There are no hot coals to clear up afterwards and they are easy to clean. Most have a flat plate and a grill rack so you can cook every cut of meat or type of fish with ease. So whether cooking for two or a large group, dinner is quick and easy.

The cheapest gas barbecue is again "table" shaped with legs and has gas burners rather than charcoal. These can have a lid and usually have both a grill and flat plate.

The slightly larger and more expensive gas barbecue on wheels come with a dome-shaped lid and often have an additional side shelf for stacking plates. They usually have a thermometer and some have a rotisserie attachment. The lid allows the barbecue to act like a conventional oven.

There is also an "all bells and whistles" version, which is more like an outdoor kitchen for the true barbecue enthusiast. They often come in stainless steel, looking quite grand and will have all the mod cons.

Gas bottles are widely available from many gas stations as well as hardware stores and

barbecue suppliers. A deposit is paid on the bottle and then it can be refilled as and when is necessary.

cooking on a barbecue

The most common cooking method on a barbecue is by the "direct grilling method." Here the food is cooked directly over a high heat (between 400–500˚F) to give it that wonderful chargrilled flavor. This can be done on all types of barbecues and is usually for smaller pieces of meat, fish, and vegetables that take less than 10 minutes to cook.

If using a charcoal barbecue, once the coals or wood are hot (they will have turned to glowing ash) and have been raked to their required position, spray the grill rack with oil away from the heat and replace over the coals. Leave for 5 minutes while the rack heats up so that the food is less likely to stick. Place the food on the rack and cook on both sides until ready.

For cooking on gas, preheat the barbecue about 15 minutes before you begin to cook. Allow to heat up and then turn the knob to the heat you require. Carefully brush or spray the grill rack or flat plate with oil and cook as per the recipe.

For larger pieces of meat and fish or fatty cuts of meat such as ribs or duck breast, the cooking method required is called "indirect grilling." This means that the food is cooked more slowly and at a lower temperature on a rack set over a roasting pan. This allows the fat from the meat to drip into a tray and not onto the flames or coals, which would cause too much smoke. This method requires a barbecue with a lid.

To cook by this method with coals or wood, rake the hot coals away from the center of the grate to the edges, leaving a cool spot in the middle. The roasting pan and rack with the meat can now be set above the cool spot. You will need a lid for this method too.

You can also indirect grill easily on a gas barbecue, providing it has at least two burners. Preheat the barbecue to hot, then turn the burners down to medium. If you have two burners, then turn one off. If you have three, turn the center one off. Place the roasting pan with the rack and meat over the unlit burner, cover, and cook as per the recipe.

To make a temporary lid, you can use the lid of a wok, which is ideal.

smoking

If the recipe requires smoking, the easiest and cheapest method is to make a smoking

pouch using foil. Take a large rectangle of foil, about 24 inches long, and fold it in half crosswise. Presoak a large handful of wood chips (which are readily available from most barbecue suppliers) in cold water for at least 30 minutes. Drain and place on one half of the foil. Fold the other side over and seal around the edges. Pierce ten or so holes into the foil with a knife. This can then be placed on the hot barbecue, either directly on the coals or wood, or directly on top of one of the gas burners beneath the actual grill rack. After a few minutes the wood will begin to smoke and you can then place the food on the oiled rack, cover with the lid and cook for the required time.

equipment

- Spray oil for spraying the food or the grill
- Long-handled tongs
- A pastry brush for basting
- Good-quality thick oven mitts
- Meat thermometer (ideal for testing if larger cuts are done)
- Matches or tapers
- Firelighters
- Sufficient fuel to last the evening
- A ridged grill pan (as an alternative to a flat plate if you have a charcoal barbecue)
- A good-quality wire brush for cleaning
- A grill basket for cooking fish or small items
- Metal or bamboo skewers for kebabs
- A torch or outdoor light for evening cooking

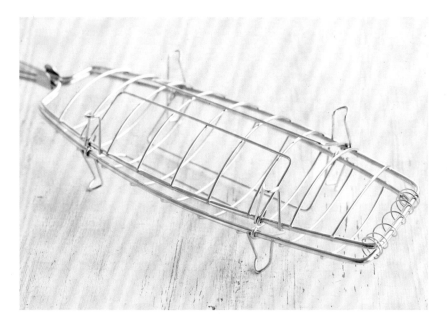

cleaning

Both charcoal and gas barbecues will need cleaning. Before cooking, use a wire brush to rub off any cooked-on bits of food from the grill rack. To avoid this at the time, though, the best time to clean the grill rack is directly after cooking while the rack is still hot. Use a wire brush to rub off as much of the cooked-on food as possible.

Always keep your barbecue dry when not in use, covered with a waterproof sheet during bad weather and through the winter.

Spraying the grill rack or flat plate with oil after cleaning will help to avoid rusting.

fire safety

• Always check that there are no weather warnings such as high winds if using charcoal or wood
• Always keep a fire extinguisher and fire blanket nearby just in case a fire does break out. Sand is the best method for putting out a ground fire, while salt will put out a grease fire on the rack

• Cook as close to the house or dining area as possible, to avoid carrying hot food long distances

• Place the barbecue in a sheltered spot where there is little or no wind to blow smoke and sparks and avoid areas with dry timbers or long, dry grass

• Place a portable barbecue on a flat, hard surface such as a patio and avoid cooking on a wooden deck

• Never leave hot coals or food, once cooking, unattended

• Do not wear open sandals when barbecuing: burns will be painful

• Always allow coals or wood to cool completely before safely and legally disposing of them. This can take up to 2 hours

food safety

• If you are marinating something for an hour or less, then it should be fine to do this in a cool place, but if in doubt, refrigerate it. If marinating overnight, always refrigerate and return to room temperature 1 hour before cooking

• If you are grilling vegetables to eat later, then try to get them to cool down as quickly as possible in a cool place, then chill in the refrigerator until required

• Always make sure that chicken and pork are thoroughly cooked through before eating. This can be done either by using a meat thermometer or by inserting a skewer into the thickest part of the meat. If the juices run clear, the meat is cooked. If they are bloody, return to the grill and continue cooking

• Remember that young children, the elderly, and pregnant women are particularly vulnerable to illness caused by unsafe foods, and the main way for food to become contaminated is by poor storage or the use of dirty utensils

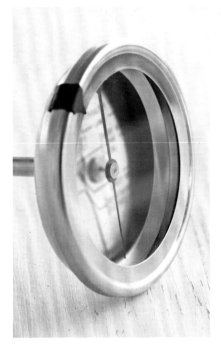

taste
tempters

shrimp & bacon skewers

Serves **4**
Preparation time **15 minutes**,
　plus marinating
Cooking time **4–6 minutes**

4 **bacon slices**, rind removed
12 raw peeled large **shrimp**,
　deveined but tails intact
12 **cherry tomatoes**
12 **basil leaves**
spray oil
salt and **black pepper**
1 **lemon**, to garnish

Soak 12 bamboo skewers in cold water for
30 minutes. Cut each bacon slice into 3 pieces
crosswise, then run the back of a knife along the
length of each piece to stretch them out thinly.

Wrap each shrimp carefully with bacon and thread on
to a soaked bamboo skewer with a tomato and basil
leaf. Season each skewer with a little salt and pepper.

Spray the skewers with a little oil and cook on a
hot barbecue for 2–3 minutes on each side until
the shrimp are cooked through. Squeeze with lemon
juice and serve hot.

For date, goat cheese, & bacon canapés, take
4 bacon slices and follow the method above to stretch
them out thinly. Slit open 12 large Medjool dates and
remove the pits. Place 1 teaspoon goat cheese into
each slit and then wrap each date with a piece of
bacon. Thread onto soaked bamboo skewers and
barbecue for 2–3 minutes on each side until the
bacon is cooked.

yakitori chicken skewers

Serves **4**

Preparation time **15 minutes**,
  plus marinating

Cooking time **4–6 minutes**

3 tablespoons **Japanese soy
  sauce**

1½ tablespoons **sake** or **dry
  sherry**

1 tablespoon **superfine sugar**

10 oz skinless **chicken thigh
  fillets**, cut lengthwise into
  ½ inch strips

5 tablespoons **Mayonnaise**
  (see page 158)

1 teaspoon **wasabi paste**

Combine the soy sauce, sake, and sugar in a small
saucepan and heat gently to dissolve the sugar. Allow
to cool completely. Place the chicken in a shallow dish,
add the marinade, and allow to marinate for at least
1 hour.

Soak 8 bamboo skewers in cold water for 30 minutes.
Mix the mayonnaise and wasabi paste together in a
bowl, then cover and set aside until required.

Thread the chicken onto the skewers and cook on
a hot barbecue for 2–3 minutes on each side until
cooked through. Serve with the wasabi mayonnaise
for dipping.

For teriyaki tuna, put 3 tablespoons soy sauce,
3 tablespoons sake, 2 tablespoons mirin (rice wine
seasoning), and 1 tablespoon superfine sugar in a
saucepan and heat gently, stirring, until the sugar
dissolves. Allow to cool completely. Marinate 4 x 5 oz
tuna steaks in the sauce for 15 minutes. Drain the
marinade back into the saucepan and simmer gently
for 2–3 minutes until thickened. Meanwhile, barbecue
the tuna fillets for 1 minute on each side and serve
drizzled with the teriyaki sauce.

spiced chicken wings

Serves **4**
Preparation time **10 minutes**,
 plus marinating
Cooking time **8–10 minutes**

8 large **chicken wings**
flat leaf parsley sprig,
 to garnish
lime wedges, to serve

Marinade
1 **garlic clove**
2 inch piece of **fresh ginger
 root**, peeled and chopped
juice and finely grated zest of
 2 **limes**
2 tablespoons **light soy sauce**
2 tablespoons **peanut oil**
2 teaspoons **ground cinnamon**
1 teaspoon **ground turmeric**
2 tablespoons **honey**
salt

Yellow pepper dip
2 **yellow bell peppers**
2 tablespoons **plain yogurt**
1 tablespoon **dark soy sauce**
1 tablespoon chopped **cilantro**
black pepper

Soak 8 bamboo skewers in cold water for 30 minutes.

Place the marinade ingredients in a blender or food processor and blend until smooth.

Arrange the chicken wings in a shallow dish, pour the marinade over, and toss to cover. Cover and allow to marinate for 1–2 hours.

Put the peppers for the dip on a hot barbecue for 10 minutes, turning occasionally, until they are charred and blistered. Remove and place in a plastic bag, then seal and leave until cool. Peel off the skins and remove the seeds and white membrane. Put the flesh into a food processor or blender with the yogurt and blend until smooth. Pour into a bowl, season with soy sauce and pepper to taste, and stir in the cilantro. Cover and chill until needed.

Remove the chicken from the marinade, thread onto the skewers and cook on a hot barbecue for 4–5 minutes on each side, basting with the remaining marinade. Garnish with a parsley sprig, then serve with the dip and some lime wedges.

For spiced shrimp, make the marinade as above, but reduce the honey to 1 teaspoon. Place in a bowl, add 20 raw peeled large shrimp and stir to combine. Allow to marinate for 30 minutes. Thread the shrimp onto soaked bamboo skewers and spray with oil. Barbecue the shrimp for 2–3 minutes on each side and serve with lime wedges.

scallop & chorizo skewers

Serves **4**

Preparation time **10 minutes**, plus marinating

Cooking time **4–6 minutes**

12 **scallops**, white meat only

12 large **sage leaves**

5 oz **chorizo sausage**, cut into 12 x ½ inch slices

2 tablespoons **extra virgin olive oil**

1 tablespoon **lemon juice**

1 **garlic clove**, crushed

salt and **black pepper**

Soak 12 small bamboo skewers in cold water for 30 minutes.

Wrap each scallop with a sage leaf and thread onto the soaked bamboo skewers with a slice of the chorizo. Mix the oil, lemon juice, garlic, and salt and pepper together and drizzle over the skewers. Marinate for 1 hour.

Cook the skewers on a hot barbecue for 2–3 minutes on each side until the scallops are cooked though. Serve at once.

For grilled scallops with pesto, take 12 scallops on the half shell and season lightly with pepper. Drizzle with a little oil and cook shell-side down on a hot barbecue for 3–4 minutes until the scallops are cooked (they will cook through the shell). Serve topped with a spoonful of Pesto (see page 158).

ham & cheese quesadillas

Serves **4–8**
Preparation time **10 minutes**
Cooking time **4–6 minutes**

4 x 9 inch **flour tortillas**
7 oz sliced **smoked ham**
2 **tomatoes**, thinly sliced
7 oz **smoked cheese**, grated
2 tablespoons **cilantro leaves**
salt and **black pepper**

Arrange 2 of the tortillas on a work surface and top with the ham, tomatoes, cheese, cilantro, and some salt and pepper. Top with the remaining tortillas, pressing down firmly. Cook one of the quesadillas on the flat plate of a hot gas barbecue for 2–3 minutes, turning halfway through, until each side is charred and crisp. (For a charcoal barbecue, use a preheated ridged grill pan instead.) Serve as below, then cook the second quesadilla.

Transfer the quesadillas to a board, cool for a second or two and then cut into wedges to serve.

For spinach & cheese quesadillas, beat together 1 ¼ cups thawed, drained, and chopped frozen spinach, 3 oz crumbled feta cheese, 1 tablespoon grated Parmesan cheese, 1 tablespoon mascarpone cheese, a little grated nutmeg, and some salt and pepper. Sandwich 4 flour tortillas with the spinach mixture and cook on a hot barbecue as in the method above. Serve in wedges.

marinated goat cheese with pitas

Serves **4–6**
Preparation time **10 minutes**,
  plus marinating
Cooking time **2 minutes**

2 x 4 oz **goat cheese logs,**
  whole, or 1 x 8 oz **goat**
  cheese log, sliced
5 tablespoons **extra virgin**
  olive oil
1 tablespoon chopped **herbs**
  of choice
1 **red birds eye chili**, seeded
  and sliced
grated zest of **1 lime**
4–6 large round **pita breads**
extra virgin olive oil, for
  brushing
1½ teaspoons **zumac** or
  dried thyme
salt and **black pepper**

Arrange the goat cheese in a shallow ceramic dish. Combine the oil, herbs, chili, lime zest, and some salt and pepper and pour over the cheese. Allow to marinate for 1 hour.

Place the pita breads on a board. Brush the tops with oil and season with the zumac, salt, and pepper. Toast, spice side up, on a hot barbecue for 1 minute, then flip and cook the spiced side for 1 minute until crisp.

Cut the bread into wedges and serve with the goat cheese and its marinade.

For garlic butter pitas, melt ¼ cup butter in a small saucepan with 1 crushed garlic clove and a little black pepper. Barbecue 4 plain pita breads for 1 minute on each side until charred and crisp. Brush the pitas with the garlic butter and serve in wedges.

baba ganoush with grilled tortillas

Serves **6**
Preparation time **10 minutes**,
    plus cooling and marinating
Cooking time **22–27 minutes**

1 **eggplant**, about 1lb
1 **garlic clove**, crushed
1 tablespoon **lemon juice**
1 tablespoon chopped
    cilantro
2 teaspoons **tahini**
pinch of **cayenne pepper**
4 x 9 inch **flour tortillas**
olive oil, for brushing
salt and **black pepper**

Wipe the eggplant, prick it all over with a fork and cook on a hot barbecue for 20–25 minutes, turning frequently, until the flesh feels soft and the skin is blackened. Set aside until cool enough to handle.

Peel and discard the skin, then mash the flesh and strain in a sieve to extract all the excess liquid. Transfer the flesh to a blender or food processor, add the garlic, lemon juice, cilantro, tahini, cayenne, and some salt and pepper and blend until fairly smooth. Transfer to a bowl, cover, and allow to marinate for several hours for the flavors to develop.

Brush the tortillas lightly with a little oil and toast on the barbecue for 1 minute on each side. Cut into strips and serve with the dip.

For grilled eggplant, tomato, & olive dip, cut a medium eggplant crosswise into ¼ inch thick slices, brush with oil, and season with salt and black pepper. Cook on a hot barbecue for 2–3 minutes each side until charred and tender. Allow to cool and dice finely. Toss the eggplant with 1 finely chopped tomato, ⅓ cup pitted black olives, chopped, 1 crushed garlic clove, 1 tablespoon chopped fresh cilantro, 2 tablespoons extra virgin olive oil, and a squeeze of lemon juice. Serve with 4 tortillas, toasted as above.

bresaola bruschetta

Serves **6**
Preparation time **5 minutes**
Cooking time **2 minutes**

6 slices of **sourdough bread**
3 ripe **tomatoes**
4 tablespoons **Smoked Garlic
Oil** (see page 196)
6 slices of **bresaola** or
prosciutto
black pepper

Toast the bread on a medium barbecue for 1 minute on each side until charred. Remove.

Cut the tomatoes in half and rub them all over one side of the charred bread slices, then drizzle generously with the garlic oil.

Place the slices tomato side up on a platter and top each one with the bresaola and some pepper. Serve drizzled with a little extra garlic oil.

For tomato bruschetta, combine 3 diced vine-ripened tomatoes, 1 crushed garlic clove, 1 tablespoon shredded basil, 1 tablespoon extra virgin olive oil, and some salt and pepper. Toast 6 slices of sourdough bread following the method above and serve topped with the tomato mixture.

melon & prosciutto salad

Serves **4–6**
Preparation time **5 minutes**

1 small **honeydew melon**,
  halved and seeded
1 small **cantaloupe melon**,
  halved and seeded
12 thin slices of **prosciutto**
mint sprigs, to garnish

Dressing
3 oz **dolcelatte cheese**
2 tablespoons **lemon juice**
5 tablespoons **milk**
2 tablespoons chopped **mint**
salt and **black pepper**

Start by making the dressing. Put the dolcelatte and lemon juice in a small bowl and mash to a paste, using a fork. Stir in the milk and mint and add salt and pepper to taste.

Slice the melons into thin wedges. Alternatively, slice just 1 of the melons and use a melon baller to scoop out the flesh of the other.

Arrange the melon on individual serving plates with the slices of prosciutto. Spoon the dressing over and around the melon, garnish with mint, and serve immediately.

For roasted pepper, chili, & basil salad, cook 3 red bell peppers on a hot barbecue for about 15 minutes, turning them every 3–4 minutes until evenly charred. Meanwhile, cook 2 large green chilies in the same way for 4–5 minutes, turning halfway through. Transfer the peppers and chilies to a plastic bag, seal and allow to cool, then peel and seed them. Put in a bowl and dress with 3 tablespoons extra virgin olive oil, 2 teaspoons sherry vinegar, 1 crushed garlic clove, salt, and pepper and serve garnished with basil leaves.

cheesy garlic bread

Serves **4**
Preparation time **5 minutes**
Cooking time **10 minutes**

1 small **French stick**
5 tablespoons **extra virgin olive oil**
1 **garlic clove**, crushed
2 teaspoons chopped **thyme**
4 oz **buffalo mozzarella cheese**, thinly sliced
salt and **black pepper**

Cut 20 slices in the French stick without going all the way through. Combine the oil, garlic, thyme, and salt and pepper in a bowl and brush the mixture all over the cut sides and the top of the bread.

Place a slice of mozzarella in between each slice of bread. Place the stick on a double layer of foil and seal loosely. Cook on a medium-hot barbecue for 5 minutes, then open the foil out (using oven mitts, as the foil will be hot) and cook for an additional 5 minutes. Serve hot.

For bread, tomato, & mozzarella skewers, cut a small French stick into 1 inch cubes and thread onto 4–6 presoaked large bamboo skewers, alternating with a cube of diced mozzarella and a cherry tomato. Place in a ceramic dish. Mix 4 tablespoons extra virgin olive oil with 1 tablespoon chopped mixed herbs and some salt and pepper. Pour the mixture over the skewers and allow to marinate for 1 hour. Cook on a medium-hot barbecue for 2–3 minutes until the cheese starts to melt.

prosciutto & asparagus parcels

Serves **4**
Preparation time **10 minutes**
Cooking time **8–10 minutes**

24 **asparagus spears**,
   trimmed
4 slices of **prosciutto**
2 Spanish **piquillo peppers**,
   drained and sliced
4 **thyme sprigs**
4 **anchovy fillets in oil**,
   drained
salt and **black pepper**
Aïoli (see page 122), to serve

Blanch the asparagus spears in lightly salted boiling water for 2 minutes. Drain well and refresh under cold water. Pat dry.

Lay a slice of prosciutto flat on a board and top with 3 asparagus spears, a slice of pepper, a thyme sprig, an anchovy fillet, and 3 more asparagus spears. Roll up into a parcel and secure with cooking string. Repeat to make 4 parcels.

Cook on a medium barbecue for 6–8 minutes, turning frequently, until evenly charred and tender. Serve the parcels with aïoli.

For grilled asparagus "soldiers," brush 20 large asparagus spears with a little oil, season, and cook on a hot barbecue for 3–4 minutes, turning halfway through, until charred and tender. Serve 5 asparagus "soldiers" per person, each with a soft-cooked egg to dip them into.

lemon grass chicken kebabs

Serves **6**
Preparation time **20 minutes**,
  plus marinating
Cooking time **8 minutes**

1 lb skinless **chicken thigh
  fillets**, cut into thin strips
2 **garlic cloves**, crushed
2 teaspoons peeled and
  grated **fresh ginger root**
1 **red birds eye chili**, seeded
  and finely chopped
grated zest of 1 **lime**
2 tablespoons **light soy
  sauce**
1 tablespoon **sesame oil**
1 teaspoon **superfine sugar**
¼ teaspoon **black pepper**
6 large **lemon grass stalks**

Place the chicken in a shallow nonmetallic dish. Combine all the remaining ingredients except for the lemon grass stalks and allow to marinate for 1 hour.

Peel and discard a few of the outer layers of the lemon grass stalks so that they are a little finer. Cut the thinner end into a point and thread the marinated chicken onto each stalk at this end, zigzagging backward and forward as you go. Cook on a hot barbecue for 3–4 minutes on each side, brushing with the marinade halfway through. Serve hot.

For chicken yogurt skewers, combine ⅔ cup Greek or whole milk yogurt with 2 teaspoons ground coriander, 1 teaspoon each ground cumin and cinnamon, 2 crushed garlic cloves, grated zest and juice of ½ lemon, 1 teaspoon honey, and some salt and pepper. Prepare 1 lb chicken thigh fillets following the method above and marinate them in the yogurt mix for 1 hour. Thread onto 6 metal skewers and grill as above. Serve with an arugula salad.

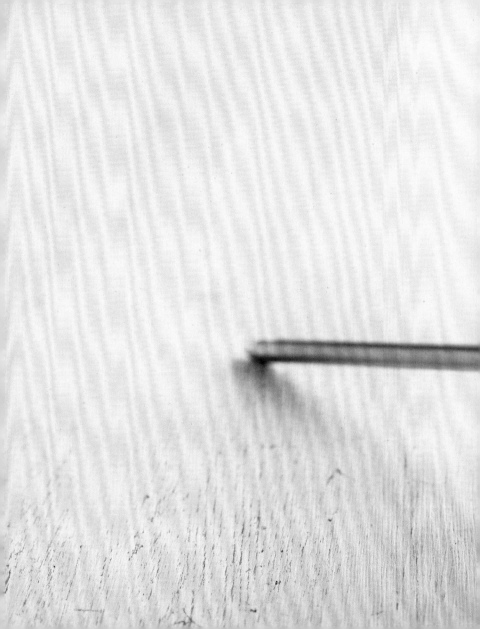

steak & ribs

herbed lamb with fig salad

Serves **4**

Preparation time **15 minutes**,
plus marinating

Cooking time **4–6 minutes**

6 tablespoons **extra virgin
olive oil**

1 quantity **Rosemary,
Coriander, & Lemon Rub**
(see page 192)

1 **garlic clove**, crushed

12 **lamb chops**

2½ cups **wild arugula**

4 **figs**, sliced

½ cup pitted **black olives**,
halved

2–3 teaspoons **lemon juice**,
to taste

salt and **black pepper**

Tahini Sauce, to serve
(see page 98)

Put 2 tablespoons of the oil, the Rosemary, Coriander,
& Lemon Rub, the garlic, and some salt and pepper in
a zip-lock bag. Add the lamb, toss well, and seal the
bag. Allow to marinate in a cool place for 1–4 hours.

Remove the lamb from the marinade and pat dry. Cook
on a hot barbecue for 2–3 minutes on each side, then
wrap loosely with foil and set aside for 5 minutes.

Meanwhile, make the salad. Put the arugula, figs, and
olives in a large bowl and mix well. Beat together the
remaining oil and 2–3 teaspoons lemon juice with
some salt and pepper. Add to the salad and stir to coat
the leaves. Serve with the lamb and some Tahini Sauce.

For lamb steaks with mint butter, combine ½ cup
softened butter with 2 tablespoons chopped mint and
some black pepper. Roll into a log, wrap in foil, and
chill for 1 hour. Season 4 x 7 oz lamb leg steaks and
cook on a hot barbecue for 3–4 minutes on each side.
Rest and serve topped with slices of the mint butter.

barbecued spare ribs

Serves **4**

Preparation time **20 minutes**,
  plus marinating

Cooking time **1 hour**
  10 minutes–1 hour
  25 minutes

2 lb **pork spare rib rack**

1 tablespoon **olive oil**, plus
  extra for brushing

4 tablespoons **Smoky**
  Barbecue Rub (see page
  194)

Barbecue sauce

1 cup **tomato paste**

½ cup **molasses**

5 tablespoons **maple syrup**

5 tablespoons **white wine**
  vinegar

2 tablespoons **Worcestershire**
  sauce

1 tablespoon **Dijon mustard**

1 teaspoon **garlic powder**

¼ teaspoon **smoked paprika**

salt and **black pepper**

Place the ribs in a large, shallow nonmetallic dish. Mix the oil and barbecue rub together and then rub this all over the ribs. Cover and allow to marinate overnight in the refrigerator.

Meanwhile, make the barbecue sauce. Place all the ingredients in a saucepan and heat gently until boiling. Simmer gently for 10–15 minutes until the sauce has thickened slightly, then set aside to cool.

Remove the ribs from the dish, brush with a little extra oil and cook on a medium barbecue for 10 minutes on each side. Brush liberally with the barbecue sauce and transfer to a rack set in a roasting pan.

Cook by indirect grilling (see page 12) for an additional 25–30 minutes on each side, basting frequently with more sauce, until charred and tender. Serve with a green salad, if desired.

For barbecued mustard & honey chicken wings,

brush 12 large chicken wings with a little oil, season with salt and pepper and cook on a medium barbecue for 15 minutes on each side. Mix 2 tablespoons dark soy sauce with 2 teaspoons Dijon mustard and 1 teaspoon honey. Brush this mixture over the wings and cook for a final 1–2 minutes on each side until glazed.

steaks with chimichurri sauce

Serves **4**
Preparation time **20 minutes**
Cooking time **6–8 minutes**

4 **rib eye steaks**, about 7 oz
  each
extra virgin olive oil, for
  brushing
salt and **black pepper**

Chimichurri sauce
bunch of **cilantro**
bunch of **parsley**
2 teaspoons **dried oregano**
2 **garlic cloves**, chopped
1 teaspoon **smoked paprika**
⅔ cup **extra virgin olive oil**
2 tablespoons **red wine**
  vinegar

Salsa
1 **avocado**, peeled, pitted,
  and diced
12 **cherry tomatoes**, halved
2 **red birds eye chilies**,
  seeded and finely chopped
2 tablespoons **cilantro leaves**
juice of ½ **lime**

Place all the chimichurri sauce ingredients in a food processor or blender and blend until fairly smooth. Season to taste and set aside until required.

Brush the steaks with a little oil and season liberally with salt and pepper. Cook on a hot barbecue for 3–4 minutes on each side or until cooked to your liking. Set aside to rest for 3 minutes.

Meanwhile, make the salsa. Put the avocado, tomatoes, chili, cilantro, lime juice, and some salt and pepper in a bowl and mix well.

Serve the steaks topped with the salsa and drizzled with the chimichurri sauce.

For steaks with salsa verde, start by making the sauce. Puree a bunch of parsley with ½ bunch each of mint, basil, and chives, a crushed garlic clove, 1 tablespoon pitted green olives, 1 tablespoon capers, 2 anchovy fillets, 1 teaspoon Dijon mustard, 2 teaspoons white wine vinegar, ⅔ cup extra virgin olive oil, and some salt and pepper. Following the method above, cook 4 rib eye steaks to your liking. Serve with the salsa verde.

tenderloin steak with tapenade

Serves **4**
Preparation time **8 minutes**
Cooking time **14–17 minutes**

¼ cup **butter**
4 **shallots**, finely chopped
1 tablespoon **wholegrain
   mustard**
1 teaspoon **Dijon mustard**
2 tablespoons **ready-made
   or homemade black olive
   tapenade** (see below)
⅔ cup **hard cider**
4 thick **tenderloin steaks**,
   about 7 oz each
2 tablespoons coarsely
   ground **black peppercorns**
2 tablespoons **sour cream**
2 tablespoons chopped
   tarragon
salt and **black pepper**

Heat the butter in a skillet until it has melted and is
beginning to froth. Add the shallots and fry gently for
5–6 minutes until softened. Add the wholegrain and
Dijon mustards and the tapenade and pour in the
cider. Simmer gently for 2 minutes, then remove
from the heat.

Press the tenderloin steaks into the black pepper.
Cook on a hot barbecue for 3–4 minutes on each side
or until cooked to your liking. Rest on warm serving
plates while finishing off the tapenade.

Stir the sour cream and tarragon into the tapenade,
season to taste with salt and pepper, and gently warm
the sauce without letting it boil. Pour a little of the
sauce over each steak and serve immediately with
steamed asparagus, homemade fries, and a dish of
mustardy mayonnaise.

For homemade tapenade sauce, combine
⅔ cup pitted black olives, 2 drained anchovy fillets,
2 crushed garlic cloves, 2 tablespoons drained
capers, 1 teaspoon Dijon mustard, 4 tablespoons
extra virgin olive oil, and a squeeze of lemon juice in
a food processor or blender and blend until smooth.
Season to taste.

steaks with garlic-herb butter

Serves **4**
Preparation time **10 minutes**,
  plus chilling
Cooking time **10 minutes**

4 **T-bone steaks**, about
  1 lb each
1½ tablespoons chopped
  thyme
2 tablespoons **extra virgin
  olive oil**
salt and **black pepper**

Garlic & parsley butter
½ cup **butter**, softened
1 **garlic clove**, crushed
2 tablespoons drained **capers**
1 tablespoon chopped
  parsley

Put the ingredients for the butter in a bowl and season to taste. Shape into a log, wrap in plastic wrap and chill until required. Cut into slices.

Season the steaks with salt, pepper, and thyme and rub with oil. Cook on a hot barbecue for 5 minutes on each side, then wrap loosely in foil and set aside to rest for 5 minutes. Serve topped with the butter.

For steaks with grilled mushrooms, season and oil 4 trimmed large field mushrooms. Cook on a hot barbecue for 5–6 minutes on each side until tender. Meanwhile, following the method above, cook 4 T-bone steaks to your liking. Rest and serve with the mushrooms, some chopped parsley, a squeeze of lemon juice, and a generous dash of extra virgin olive oil.

hoisin ribs

Serves **4**
Preparation time **25 minutes**
Cooking time **65–70 minutes**

2 lb **pork spare rib rack**
4 tablespoons **white wine vinegar**
sliced **scallions**, to garnish

Hoisin barbecue sauce
3 tablespoons **hoisin sauce**
3 tablespoons **tomato ketchup**
2 tablespoons **white wine vinegar**
2 tablespoons **dark soy sauce**
2 tablespoons **honey**
1 large **garlic clove**, crushed
1 teaspoon freshly peeled and grated **fresh ginger root**
1 teaspoon **sesame oil**
½ teaspoon **Chinese five-spice powder**

Place the ribs in a large saucepan with the vinegar and add enough water to cover by a good 2 inches. Bring to a boil and simmer for 20 minutes. Drain the ribs and dry on paper towels. Transfer to a bowl.

Meanwhile, place all the sauce ingredients in a saucepan and bring just to a boil. Simmer gently for 6–8 minutes until thickened slightly.

Brush the ribs with the marinade and, using the indirect grilling method (see page 12), cook on a medium barbecue for 45–50 minutes, basting and turning frequently until the ribs are glazed and tender. Serve with steamed rice.

For hoisin salmon steaks, make the sauce as above and allow to cool. Brush 4 x 7 oz salmon steaks with a little of the sauce and cook on a medium barbecue for 3–4 minutes on each side. Serve with a crisp green salad.

rum & maple pork belly

Serves **6**
Preparation time **5 minutes**,
  plus marinating
Cooking time **1 hour 40
  minutes–1 hour 50
  minutes**

2 lb piece of **pork belly**, skin
  and ribs removed, or same
  weight **pork belly slices**
1 tablespoon **olive oil**
2–4 tablespoons **jerk spice
  seasoning**

Rum & maple glaze
½ cup **maple syrup**
½ cup **light brown sugar**
4 tablespoons **dark rum**
juice of 1 **orange**
2 tablespoons **red wine
  vinegar**
½ teaspoon **ground cinnamon**
salt and **pepper**

Place the pork belly in a ceramic dish and brush with oil. Rub the jerk seasoning all over the pork and marinate overnight in the refrigerator. Return to room temperature 1 hour before cooking and remove from the marinade.

Cook the pork belly on a hot barbecue for 10 minutes each side until browned, then transfer to a rack set over a roasting pan. Cook by indirect grilling method (see page 12) for 1 hour.

Meanwhile, make the glaze. Place all the ingredients in a saucepan and heat gently until the sugar is dissolved. Simmer gently for 10 minutes until the glaze is thick and syrup-like.

Brush the pork belly with the glaze and cook for an additional 10–15 minutes each side until it is fully glazed and meltingly tender.

For new potato salad, to serve as an accompaniment, cook 1½ lb scrubbed new potatoes until tender. Drain well, mash very lightly to break the potatoes up a little, and stir in 4 tablespoons good-quality mayonnaise, 4 trimmed and finely sliced scallions, 2 tablespoons snipped chives, 1 tablespoon white wine vinegar, 2 teaspoons wholegrain mustard, and some salt and pepper. Allow to cool.

fennel pork with tarragon butter

Serves **4**
Preparation time **5 minutes,**
  plus chilling
Cooking time **8–10 minutes**

4 **pork loin chops,** about
  8 oz each
1 tablespoon **olive oil**
2 tablespoons **Fennel Rub**
  (see page 192)
lemon wedges, to serve

Tarragon butter
½ cup **butter**
2 tablespoons chopped
  tarragon
salt and **black pepper**

Brush the pork chops with oil, rub in the spice mixture and then place in a shallow dish. Allow to marinate in a cool place for 2 hours.

Meanwhile, beat the butter, tarragon, and some pepper together until well blended. Roll into a log and wrap in plastic wrap, then chill until required.

Cook the steaks on a hot barbecue for 4–5 minutes on each side, then wrap loosely in foil and set aside to rest for 5 minutes. Cut the butter into slices and serve atop the steaks, with lemon wedges alongside.

For chargrilled salmon with tarragon butter, lightly season 4 x 7 oz salmon fillets, brush with oil, and barbecue on a high heat for 3–4 minutes on each side. Rest briefly and serve topped with slices of tarragon butter, following the recipe above.

prosciutto-wrapped beef

Serves **8**

Preparation time **30 minutes**

Cooking time **25 minutes**,
plus resting

2 tablespoons chopped
thyme

grated zest of 2 **lemons**

4 tablespoons **extra virgin
olive oil**

2 **beef eye fillets**, about
1½ lb each

12 large slices of **prosciutto**

4 large **potatoes**, about
2½ lb total weight

salt and **black pepper**

Mix the thyme, lemon zest, 2 tablespoons of the oil,
and some salt and pepper together and rub it all over
the beef fillet. Wrap the prosciutto around the beef to
flavor it and keep it moist, and secure in place with
cooking string.

Cook on the flat plate of a hot gas barbecue for
25 minutes, turning frequently (or use the indirect
grilling method for a charcoal barbecue). Remove the
beef, wrap in a double layer of foil, and set aside to
rest for 20 minutes.

Meanwhile, cut the potatoes lengthwise into ½ inch
thick slices and parboil for 5 minutes. Drain well, brush
with the remaining oil, and season with salt and pepper.
Cook the potato slices on the grill rack for 3–4 minutes
on each side until charred and tender.

Slice the beef and serve with the potatoes and a
spinach salad (see below).

For spinach salad, to serve as an accompaniment,
wash and drain 2½ cups baby spinach leaves and
place in a bowl. Beat together 2 tablespoons extra
virgin olive oil, 2 teaspoons red wine vinegar, a pinch
of superfine sugar, and some salt and pepper. Pour
the dressing over the salad, toss well, and serve.

moroccan chicken & salad

Serves: **4–6**
Preparation time **15 minutes**,
  plus marinating
Cooking time **12–16 minutes**

4 **chicken breast fillets** with
  skin, about 8 oz each
2 tablespoons **pomegranate
  molasses** (or 2 tablespoons
  honey mixed with
  1 teaspoon **lemon juice**)
1 tablespoon **extra virgin
  olive oil**
2 teaspoons **zumac** or
  dried thyme
salt and **black pepper**

Moroccan salad
1 small **eggplant**
2 tablespoons **extra virgin
  olive oil**
2 **flatbreads**
8 oz **cherry tomatoes**,
  quartered
1 **Lebanese cucumber**, diced
½ cup pitted **black olives**,
  chopped
½ bunch each **mint, cilantro,**
  and **parsley leaves**
1 **pomegranate**, peeled
juice of ½ **lemon**
1 teaspoon **superfine sugar**

Score the skin side of each chicken breast several times and place in a bowl. Add the pomegranate molasses, oil, zumac, and a generous sprinkling of salt and pepper. Rub into the chicken and allow to marinate in a cool place for 1 hour.

Remove the chicken from the marinade, reserving the juices, and cook on a medium-hot barbecue for 6–8 minutes on each side until charred and cooked through. Set aside to rest for 5 minutes.

Heat the reserved marinade juices in a small pan until boiling and reduced slightly. Brush over the cooked chicken to glaze.

Meanwhile, make the salad. Cut the eggplant crosswise into ¼ inch thick slices. Brush with a little of the oil and cook on a hot barbecue for 1–2 minutes each side. Toast the flatbreads on the barbecue for 30 seconds or so on each side until crisp, then crumble into a large bowl. Add the tomatoes, cucumber, olives, herbs, and pomegranate seeds. Beat the remaining oil, lemon juice, sugar, and a little salt and pepper and add to the salad. Toss well and serve with the chicken.

For pomegranate chicken wings, follow the above recipe, replacing the chicken breast with 12 large wings. Marinate for 1 hour and cook on a medium-hot barbecue for 10–12 minutes on each side. Cool for 5 minutes before serving with a crisp green salad.

butterflied citrus chicken

Serves **4**
Preparation time **15 minutes**
Cooking time **40 minutes**

3 lb **chicken**
2 tablespoons **extra virgin olive oil**
salt and **black pepper**

Grilled lemon dressing
3 **lemons**, halved
spray oil
1 **garlic clove**, crushed
5 tablespoons **extra virgin olive oil**
pinch of **superfine sugar**
1 large **red chili**, seeded and finely chopped
2 tablespoons chopped **parsley**

Ask your butcher to butterfly the chicken for you, or do it yourself if you know how.

Season the chicken with salt and pepper and rub with the oil. Thread two metal skewers through the bird diagonally (from wing tip to drumstick) to keep flat. Cook on a hot barbecue, breast-side down, for 5 minutes, then lower the heat to medium and cook, covered, for 15 minutes. Turn the chicken over and cook for an additional 20 minutes. Set aside to rest for 10 minutes.

Meanwhile, spray the cut face of the lemon halves with a little oil and place them, cut-side down, on a hot barbecue. Cook for 10 minutes, turning frequently, until charred and softened. Set aside to cool.

Squeeze the lemon juice from two lemon halves into a bowl and stir in the garlic, oil, sugar, chili, parsley, and salt and pepper to taste.

Transfer the cooked bird to a board, cut into large pieces using a big knife and place on a warmed platter. Pour the dressing over it and serve garnished with some chili, parsley, and the remaining lemon halves.

For watercress, lamb's lettuce, & almond salad, to serve as an accompaniment, toast ¾ cup blanched almonds in a preheated oven, 375°F, for 5–6 minutes until evenly browned. Set aside to cool. Combine 1¼ cups watercress leaves, 1¼ cups lamb's lettuce, the almonds, and ½ cup golden raisins in a bowl. Drizzle a little oil and a dash of balsamic vinegar over, season with salt and pepper, and stir. Serve with the chicken.

lamb with beet & feta salad

Serves **4**

Preparation time **15 minutes**, plus marinating

Cooking time **40–45 minutes**

2 **lamb loins**, about 8 oz each
1 tablespoon **extra virgin olive oil**
1 tablespoon **dried oregano**
1 lb small **beets**
7 oz **green beans**, trimmed
4 oz **feta cheese**
2 cups **baby spinach leaves**
1 cup **walnuts**, toasted
salt and **black pepper**

Walnut oil & raspberry dressing
3 tablespoons **walnut oil**
2–3 teaspoons **raspberry vinegar**
2 teaspoons **wholegrain mustard**

Brush the lamb loins with the oil and rub with the oregano and some salt and pepper. Set aside to marinate for 1 hour.

Meanwhile, place the beets in a saucepan of cold water, bring to a boil, and cook for 20 minutes until just tender. Drain well, cut into wedges, and place in a bowl. Add a little oil and thread onto 2 metal skewers. Cook on a hot barbecue for 6–8 minutes on each side until lightly charred. Return to the bowl.

Blanch the beans in lightly salted boiling water for 3 minutes. Drain, refresh under cold water, and dry well. Add to the beets with the feta, spinach, and walnuts.

Beat the dressing ingredients and some salt and pepper together in a small bowl.

Cook the lamb on a hot barbecue for 4–5 minutes on each side, then set aside to rest briefly. Serve in slices with the salad, drizzled with the dressing.

For chargrilled loin chops with mint dressing, lightly season 8 x 4 oz loin chops, brush with a little oil, and cook on a hot barbecue for 3–4 minutes on each side. Rest briefly. Meanwhile, beat together 2 tablespoons chopped mint, 5 tablespoons white wine vinegar, 2 tablespoons extra virgin olive oil, 2 teaspoons superfine sugar, and some salt and pepper. Drizzle over the chops and serve with a simple green salad.

steak with mustardy fries

Serves **4**
Preparation time **10 minutes**
Cooking time **20 minutes**

1 lb **potatoes**, scrubbed
3 tablespoons **olive oil**
1 **egg white**
1 teaspoon **wholegrain mustard**
½ teaspoon **ground turmeric**
8 oz **cherry tomatoes**
8 oz **closed cup mushrooms**, trimmed
4 thick-cut **sirloin steaks**, about 7 oz each, trimmed
black pepper

Parboil the potatoes for 5 minutes, then drain. Cut in half lengthwise, then cut into chunky wedges. Put 1 tablespoon of the oil in a bowl, add the egg white, mustard, turmeric, and a little pepper and fork together until the egg white is slightly frothy. Add the potatoes and toss well.

Arrange the potato wedges in a single layer on the flat plate of a hot gas barbecue or in a ridged pan on a charcoal barbecue and cook for 10 minutes. Add the tomatoes and cook for 5 more minutes or until the fries are golden and the tomato skins just beginning to split.

Meanwhile, brush the mushrooms and steaks with the remaining oil and sprinkle the steaks with a little pepper. Cook the steaks on the barbecue for 3–4 minutes on each side, or until cooked to your liking. Set aside to rest for 5 minutes while cooking the mushrooms.

Transfer the steak, fries, and vegetables to serving plates and serve immediately.

For watercress salad, to serve as an accompaniment, combine 2½ cups watercress leaves with 1¼ cups frisée leaves in a large bowl and add ½ cup toasted walnuts. Mix together 2 teaspoons white wine vinegar, 2 teaspoons wholegrain mustard, ½ teaspoon superfine sugar, and some salt and pepper in a bowl and beat in 3 tablespoons walnut oil. Pour over the salad and stir to combine.

kebabs, burgers, & hot dogs

hot dogs with barbecue sauce

Serves **4**
Preparation time **10 minutes**
Cooking time **15–20 minutes**

2 large **onions**, sliced
2 tablespoons **extra virgin
    olive oil**
1 tablespoon chopped **thyme**
4 large **pork sausages**
4 **hot dog rolls**, halved
a little **butter**
4 tablespoons **Barbecue
    Sauce** (see page 46)
salt and **black pepper**

Toss the onions with the oil, thyme, salt, and pepper, then cook on the flat plate of a hot gas barbecue for 15–20 minutes until soft and golden. (For a charcoal barbecue, use a preheated ridged grill pan instead.)

Meanwhile, cook the sausages on the barbecue until lightly charred and cooked through, about 10 minutes.

Butter the bread rolls and fill with the sausages, onions, and a tablespoon of barbecue sauce.

For mustard & pickle dogs, cook the sausages and onions as in the recipe above. Serve in 4 hot dog rolls topped with 2 medium dill pickles, diced, and a drizzle of classic American mustard.

chicken & mozzarella skewers

Serves **4**
Preparation time **25 minutes**
Cooking time **16 minutes**

8 small boneless **chicken
 thigh fillets**, skinned
2 **bocconcini balls** (baby
 mozzarellas), quartered
8 large **basil leaves**
8 large slices of **prosciutto**
2 small **lemons**, halved
salt and **black pepper**

Lay the chicken thighs flat with the boned side facing upward. Season each one with a little salt and pepper. Place one-quarter of a bocconcini and a basil leaf in the center of each one and roll the chicken up to enclose the filling. Wrap each thigh in a slice of prosciutto and thread onto 8 metal skewers, allowing 2 skewers per 2 parcels (making them easy to turn).

Cook the skewers on the flat plate of a hot gas barbecue for 8 minutes on each side until the mozzarella starts to ooze. (For a charcoal barbecue, cook directly on the rack.) Wrap in foil and set aside to rest for 5 minutes. Take care when handling the skewers as they will be very hot.

Meanwhile, cook the lemon halves, cut-side down, for 5 minutes until charred and tender.

Serve the skewers drizzled with the lemon juice.

For arugula & Parmesan salad, to serve as an accompaniment, put 2½ cups baby arugula leaves in a bowl and season lightly with salt and pepper. Beat together 2 tablespoons extra virgin olive oil, 1 teaspoon balsamic vinegar, and some salt and pepper. Drizzle a little of the dressing over the arugula, toss well, and serve sprinkled with ½ oz shaved Parmesan.

classic hamburger

Serves **4**
Preparation time **10 minutes**,
  plus chilling
Cooking time **10–12 minutes**

1 lb **rib eye steak**, ground
8 oz skinless **pork belly**,
  ground
1 **onion**, finely chopped
1 teaspoon **Worcestershire
  sauce**
2 tablespoons drained **capers**
olive oil, for brushing
4 **hamburger buns**, halved
2 tablespoons **mustard**
4 cups shredded **lettuce
  leaves**
2 **tomatoes**, sliced
2 **dill pickles**, sliced
salt and **black pepper**

Put the ground beef and pork in a bowl with the onion, Worcestershire sauce, capers, salt, and pepper. Mix together well, using your hands. Divide the mixture into quarters and shape into 4 even-size patties. Chill for 30 minutes.

Brush the patties with oil and cook on a hot barbecue for 5–6 minutes on each side until lightly charred on the outside while just cooked through inside.

Meanwhile, toast the buns on the barbecue for 1 minute on the cut side.

Spread the insides of the buns with a little mustard, fill with the shredded lettuce, patties, tomato slices, and dill pickles.

For beef burgers with grilled onions, follow the recipe above, omitting the pork and using 1½ lb ground steak. Combine the beef with 1 finely chopped onion, 4 finely chopped anchovies, 2 tablespoons chopped parsley, and some salt and pepper. Shape into patties, cook, and serve topped with some browned onions (see page 72).

cheeseburger

Serves **4**
Preparation time **15 minutes**,
  plus chilling
Cooking time **10–12 minutes**

1½ lb **rib eye steak**, ground
1 **onion**, finely chopped
1 **garlic clove**, crushed
2 teaspoons chopped **thyme**
olive oil, for brushing
1 cup grated **cheddar cheese**
4 **burger buns**, halved
4 large **butter lettuce leaves**
2 **tomatoes**, sliced
salt and **black pepper**

Put the beef, onion, garlic, thyme, and some salt and pepper in a bowl. Using your hands, work them together until evenly combined and slightly sticky. Divide the mixture into quarters and shape into 4 even-size patties. Chill for 30 minutes.

Brush the patties with a little oil and cook on a hot barbecue for 5–6 minutes on each side until cooked through and lightly charred on the outside. Top the burgers with cheese and place under a hot broiler for 30 seconds until melted.

Meanwhile, toast the buns on the barbecue for 1 minute on the cut side.

Fill each bun with the lettuce leaves, cheese-topped patties, and tomato slices.

For Stilton-stuffed burgers, cut 2 oz Stilton cheese into 4 pieces. Make 4 patties following the recipe above, shaping each one around a piece of Stilton, so that it is well hidden in the center. Cook as above and serve in 4 toasted whole-wheat buns with a little watercress and some mayonnaise.

sicilian burgers

Serves **4**
Preparation time **20 minutes**,
  plus chilling
Cooking time **12–14 minutes**

1 tablespoon **olive oil**
1 **red onion**, finely chopped
3 **garlic cloves**, finely chopped
1¼ lb good-quality **coarsely
  ground beef**
2 tablespoons chopped **basil**
2 tablespoons chopped
  marjoram
2 tablespoons chopped **oregano**
½ cup freshly grated
  Parmesan cheese
⅓ cup **sun-dried tomatoes**,
  finely chopped
½ cup **black olives**, finely
  chopped
a little **olive oil**, for brushing
2 soft **focaccia rolls**,
  quartered, then halved
Mayonnaise (see page 158),
  flavored with 4 tablespoons
  chopped **basil** per quantity
2 cups **arugula**
1 ball of **mozzarella cheese**,
  about 4 oz
small bunch of **basil**
salt and **black pepper**

Heat the oil in a skillet and fry the onion and garlic over a medium heat for 4 minutes or until softened. Set aside to cool.

Place the beef, onion and garlic mixture, herbs, Parmesan, tomatoes, and olives in a large bowl, season with salt and pepper and mix well. Divide the mixture into eighths and shape into 8 even-size patties. Cover and chill for 30 minutes.

Brush the patties with a little oil and cook on a hot barbecue for 4–5 minutes on each side until slightly charred on the outside and medium in the center.

Meanwhile, toast the halved focaccia quarters on the barbecue for 1 minute on each side until browned.

Spread the base of each bun with some basil mayonnaise and top with some of the arugula and a cooked patty. Tear the mozzarella ball into pieces and divide among the 8 burgers. Top with the lids and a basil leaf and secure with a toothpick. Serve with extra basil mayonnaise and arugula, if desired.

For beet & horseradish burgers, make and cook the patties as above. Combine 1 tablespoon creamed horseradish with ⅔ cup sour cream and some salt and pepper. Place the patties in 2 large halved rolls with some sliced cooked beet, a handful of arugula leaves, and a spoonful of the horseradish cream. Cut the rolls into quarters and serve.

thai chicken burgers

Serves **4**

Preparation time **20 minutes**, plus chilling

Cooking time **14–16 minutes**

1 lb skinless **chicken breast fillets**, ground

1–2 tablespoons **Thai red curry paste**

1 small **onion**, finely chopped

2 tablespoons chopped **cilantro**

olive oil, for brushing

4 **oval buns**, halved

1 cup mixed **Asian salad leaves**

handful of mixed **Thai** or **plain basil, cilantro,** and **mint leaves**

Coconut satay sauce

6 tablespoons **coconut cream**

3 tablespoons **smooth peanut butter**

juice of ½ **lime**

2 teaspoons **Thai fish sauce**

2 teaspoons **sweet chili sauce**

Place the chicken, curry paste, onion, cilantro, and some salt and pepper in a food processor or blender and blend until smooth. Transfer to a bowl and chill for 30 minutes. Divide the mixture into quarters and shape into 8 even-size patties.

Meanwhile, put all the satay sauce ingredients in a small saucepan and heat gently, stirring until combined. Simmer gently for 1–2 minutes until thickened, then set aside to cool.

Brush the patties lightly with oil and cook on a hot barbecue for 5–6 minutes on each side until cooked through. Test one by inserting a skewer into the center: it should feel hot to the touch when the burger is cooked.

Fill the buns with the chicken burgers, Asian salad leaves, and mixed herbs and spoon the coconut satay sauce over the top.

For quick chicken fillet burgers with sweet chili sauce, cut 2 large skinless chicken breast fillets in half horizontally to give 4 thinner fillets. Season with salt and pepper, brush with oil, and cook on a hot barbecue for 4–5 minutes on each side. Squeeze over the juice of 1 lime and pop into 4 toasted buns with some salad leaves, herbs, and sweet chili sauce.

pork burgers with grilled pears

Serves **4**
Preparation time **5 minutes**
Cooking time **20 minutes**

2 tablespoons **butter**
2 **pears**, cut into quarters
6 tablespoons **maple syrup**
1 tablespoon **red wine vinegar**
1 tablespoon **wholegrain mustard**
2 teaspoons peeled and grated **fresh ginger root**
1 tablespoon chopped **sage leaves**
4 **pork tenderloin medallions**, about 4 oz each
4 **soft rolls**, halved
salad leaves
salt and **black pepper**

Heat the butter in a skillet, add the pears and fry until lightly browned. Add 2 tablespoons of the maple syrup and cook until lightly caramelized. Transfer to a roasting dish and bake in a preheated oven, 400°F, for 10 minutes or until cooked through. Keep warm until needed.

Meanwhile, beat together the remaining maple syrup with the vinegar, mustard, ginger, sage, and a little salt and pepper in a small bowl until they form a sauce.

Place the pork medallions on a hot barbecue and brush with the sauce. Cook for 4–5 minutes on each side, basting with the sauce at regular intervals, until the pork is glossy and cooked through.

Toast the rolls on the barbecue for 1 minute on each side until browned. Fill each one with salad leaves, a pork steak, and some of the baked pears.

For maple syrup-glazed pork tenderloin, combine 1 tablespoon maple syrup with 2 tablespoons olive oil, 1 tablespoon wholegrain mustard, 2 teaspoons ground coriander, and some salt and pepper. Brush this over 2 x 13 oz pork tenderloins and allow to marinate for 1 hour. Remove the pork from the marinade, cut in half crosswise, and cook on a medium-hot barbecue for 10–12 minutes, turning halfway, until cooked. Allow to rest for 5 minutes, then serve in slices with a green salad.

minted lamb kebabs

Serves **4**

Preparation time **15 minutes**, plus chilling

Cooking time **6–8 minutes**

1 lb boneless **leg of lamb**, ground

1 small **onion**, finely chopped

1 **garlic clove**, crushed

1 tablespoon chopped **rosemary**

6 **anchovies in oil**, drained and chopped

olive oil, for brushing

salt and **black pepper**

Tomato & olive salad

6 ripe **tomatoes**, cut into wedges

1 **red onion**, sliced

⅔ cup pitted **black olives**

a few torn **basil leaves**

2 tablespoons **extra virgin olive oil**

a squeeze of **lemon juice**

Combine the lamb, onion, garlic, rosemary, anchovies, and some salt and pepper in a bowl and use your hands to work them together. Divide into 12 and shape into even-size, sausage-shaped patties. Chill for 30 minutes.

Thread the patties onto metal skewers, brush lightly with oil, and barbecue for 3–4 minutes on each side until cooked through. Keep warm.

Meanwhile, make the salad. Combine the tomatoes, onion, olives, and basil in a bowl and season with salt and pepper. Drizzle with oil and squeeze a little lemon juice over. Serve the kebabs with the salad.

For lamb souvlaki, cube 1½ lb lamb shoulder and place in a bowl. Add 1¼ cups red wine, 2 tablespoons red wine vinegar, 1 chopped onion, 2 chopped garlic cloves, 2 tablespoons dried oregano, 1 tablespoon extra virgin olive oil, and a little salt and pepper and allow to marinate for at least 4 hours. Remove the meat from the marinade and thread onto skewers. Cook on a hot barbecue for 4–5 minutes on each side and serve with the salad and some tzatziki.

breakfast burger with mushrooms

Serves **4**
Preparation time **15 minutes**,
  plus chilling
Cooking time **10–12 minutes**

1½ lb boneless **pork
  shoulder**, ground
2 **garlic cloves**, crushed
1 tablespoon chopped **thyme**
2 tablespoons **cornstarch**
1 **egg**, lightly beaten
spray oil
4 large **flat mushrooms**,
  trimmed
4 **Canadian bacon slices**,
  rind removed
4 large **sesame seed rolls**,
  halved
2 ripe **tomatoes**, sliced
American-style mustard or
  mayonnaise (optional)
salt and **black pepper**
tomato sauce, to serve

Combine the pork, garlic, thyme, cornstarch, egg, and some salt and pepper in a bowl and, using your hands, work together until well blended. Divide the mixture into quarters and shape into 4 even-size patties. Chill for 30 minutes.

Spray the patties with a little oil and cook on a hot barbecue for 5–6 minutes on each side. Set aside to rest until required. Barbecue the mushrooms for 2–3 minutes on each side and the bacon for 2 minutes on each side.

Place the patties on the sesame rolls and top with the mushrooms, bacon, and tomatoes and some mustard, if desired. Serve with tomato sauce.

For vegetarian breakfast burgers, cook 4 large flat mushrooms as above and keep warm. Cook 2 halved tomatoes for 30 seconds on each side. Fry 4 free-range eggs in a little oil on the flat plate of a gas barbecue or in a skillet for charcoal. Arrange the mushrooms, grilled tomatoes, and fried eggs in 4 whole-wheat buns and serve with some baby spinach leaves and a spoonful of Pesto (see page 158).

barbecued pork sandwich

Serves **8**
Preparation time **45 minutes**,
   plus marinating
Cooking time **1–1¼ hours**

2 tablespoons **Smoky
   Barbecue Rub** (see
   page 194)
2 lb **boneless pork shoulder**
8 **bread rolls**

Coleslaw
2 cups shredded **white
   cabbage**
1 cup grated **carrots**
½ **white onion**, thinly sliced
1 teaspoon **salt**
2 teaspoons **superfine sugar**
1 tablespoon **white wine
   vinegar**
5 tablespoons **mayonnaise**
black pepper

Rub the spice rub into the pork and allow to marinate
overnight in the refrigerator. Return the pork to room
temperature for 1 hour before cooking.

Make the coleslaw when you are ready to cook.
Put the cabbage, carrots, and onion in a colander and
sprinkle with the salt, sugar, and vinegar. Stir well, then
allow to drain over a bowl for 30 minutes. Squeeze out
any excess liquid from the vegetables and place in a
large bowl. Mix the mayonnaise into the cabbage
mixture and season with pepper to taste. Set aside
until required.

Cook the pork by the indirect grilling method (see
page 12) on a medium barbecue for 1–1¼ hours
until tender. Wrap loosely in foil and set aside to rest
for 15 minutes. Finely slice the pork and serve in rolls
with the coleslaw.

**For barbecued pork chops with grilled apple
wedges**, season 4 x 8 oz pork chops with salt and
pepper and cook on a medium-hot barbecue for
4–5 minutes on each side. Wrap in foil and set
aside to rest for 3 minutes. Meanwhile, cut 2 cored
apples into large wedges, spray with oil, and grill for
1 minute on each side until golden and cooked. Serve
the chops with the grilled apples and a green salad.

pancetta hot dogs with salsa rossa

Serves **4**
Preparation time **15 minutes**
Cooking time **35 minutes**

6 slices of **smoked pancetta**
12 small **Italian sausages** or
  chipolatas
1 large **onion**, cut into 8 thick
  wedges
12 large **bay leaves**

Salsa rossa
1 large **red bell pepper**
1 tablespoon **extra virgin
  olive oil**
2 **garlic cloves**, crushed
2 large ripe **tomatoes**, peeled
  and roughly chopped
½ teaspoon **cayenne pepper**
1 tablespoon **red wine
  vinegar**
salt and **black pepper**

Start by making the salsa rossa. Cook the pepper
on a hot barbecue until charred all over, then put in
a plastic bag, seal, and allow to cool. When cool, peel
and discard the seeds, reserving any juices, and chop
the flesh.

Heat the oil in a pan, sauté the garlic for 3 minutes,
then add the tomatoes and cayenne pepper and
simmer gently for 15 minutes. Stir in the peppers and
the vinegar, season with salt and pepper, and simmer
for an additional 5 minutes to cook off the excess
liquid. Puree in a food processor or blender until
smooth, then set aside.

Cut the pancetta slices in half crosswise and wrap
each half around 1 sausage. Thread onto 4 large metal
skewers, alternating with the wedges of onion and bay
leaves, so that each skewer has 3 sausages, 2 onion
wedges, and 3 bay leaves. Cook on a hot barbecue for
5 minutes until charred and cooked through. Serve with
the salsa rossa, reheated if necessary.

For chargrilled chicken & salsa rossa sandwiches,
cut 2 chicken breast fillets in half crosswise to give
4 thin fillets and season well. Cook on a hot barbecue
for 4–5 minutes on each side, then set aside to rest
for 3 minutes. Lightly toast 4 burger buns and fill each
with a chicken fillet, some salsa rossa, and ½ cup
arugula leaves for each roll.

shish kebabs

Serves **6**
Preparation time **15 minutes**,
 plus marinating
Cooking time **10–15 minutes**

12 oz **ground lamb**
1 **onion**, finely chopped
2 teaspoons **lemon juice**
1 **egg**, beaten
2 tablespoons **all-purpose
 flour**
2 tablespoons chopped
 cilantro
½ teaspoon **salt**
oil, for brushing

Marinade
4 tablespoons **plain yogurt**
1 tablespoon **medium** or **hot
 curry powder**
1 **garlic clove**, crushed

To garnish
red onion, finely sliced
red bell pepper, finely sliced
1 tablespoon chopped
 parsley
1 teaspoon **paprika**
lime wedges

Mix all the ingredients except for the oil in a large bowl
until smooth. Divide the mixture into 6 and form into
even-size, sausage-shaped patties.

Make the marinade. Mix the yogurt, curry powder,
and garlic in a flat-based dish. Thread the patties
onto oiled metal skewers and allow to marinate for
2–4 hours.

Remove the skewers from the marinade. Brush the
patties with oil and cook on a medium-hot barbecue
for 10–15 minutes, turning occasionally.

Serve hot, garnished with the onion, pepper, and
parsley, dusted over with paprika, and with lime
wedges to squeeze over.

For shish kebab pitas, make and cook the patties
as above, then stuff into 6 warmed pita breads with
shredded lettuce, sliced tomatoes, and some Tahini
Sauce (see page 98).

angler fish & shrimp kebabs

Serves **4**

Preparation time **15 minutes**,
   plus soaking and marinating

Cooking time **4–6 minutes**

8 large **rosemary sprigs**

1 lb **angler fish fillets**, cut
   into 16 large chunks

16 raw peeled **jumbo shrimp**,
   deveined

2 **garlic cloves**, crushed

grated zest and juice of
   1 lemon

1½ tablespoons **extra virgin
   olive oil**

1 recipe quantity **Aïoli**
   (see page 122) with
   1 tablespoon **lemon juice**
   added with the egg yolks

Rip the rosemary leaves from the stalks, leaving a few rosemary leaves on the end of each sprig. Cut the other end on a diagonal to form a sharp tip. Soak in cold water for 30 minutes. Finely chop 1 tablespoon of the rosemary leaves, reserving the rest for another dish.

Thread the fish chunks onto the soaked rosemary skewers, alternating with the shrimp, allowing 2 cubes of fish and 2 shrimp per skewer. Place in a shallow nonmetallic dish.

Combine the chopped rosemary, garlic, lemon zest, and some salt and black pepper with the oil, pour over the kebabs and allow to marinate for 1 hour. Remove from the marinade. Cook on a hot barbecue for 2–3 minutes on each side until cooked, squeeze the lemon juice over the kebabs, and serve with the lemon aïoli.

For grilled angler fish wrapped in prosciutto, wrap 4 x 7 oz angler fish fillets in a large slice of prosciutto each and secure with toothpicks. Brush with oil and cook on a hot barbecue for 5–6 minutes, turning halfway through. Allow to rest for 5 minutes, then serve with aïoli and an arugula salad.

swordfish kebabs with tahini sauce

Serves **4**
Preparation time **20 minutes**,
  plus marinating
Cooking time **4–6 minutes**

2 lb **swordfish steaks**, cubed
2 teaspoons **ground turmeric**
1 teaspoon **ground cinnamon**
grated zest of 1 **lemon**
2 tablespoons **extra virgin
  olive oil**
8 x 9 inch **flour tortillas**
2½ cups **salad leaves**
4 ripe **tomatoes**, cut into
  wedges
a few **mint leaves**, torn
salt and **black pepper**

Tahini sauce
⅔ cup **Greek-style or whole
  milk yogurt**
2 teaspoons **tahini**
1 teaspoon **lemon juice**
1 small **garlic clove**, crushed

Soak 8 double prong bamboo skewers in cold water
for 30 minutes (you can use normal bamboo skewers,
if preferred). Place the swordfish in a shallow bowl, rub
in the turmeric, cinnamon, lemon zest, oil, and some salt
and pepper and allow to marinate for 15 minutes.
Thread onto the skewers and cook over hot coals for
2–3 minutes on each side.

Meanwhile, place the tahini sauce ingredients in a
bowl and stir well until combined. Season to taste
with salt and pepper.

Arrange half the flour tortillas on plates and top
with salad leaves, tomatoes, mint, the fish skewers,
and some tahini sauce. Wrap and push to one side.
Repeat with the remaining tortillas and filling ingredients,
then serve.

For grilled swordfish sandwiches, season 4 x 7 oz
swordfish steaks with salt and pepper and barbecue
for 1–1½ minutes on each side. Meanwhile, lightly
toast 8 slices of sourdough bread. Cover half the
slices with the swordfish steaks, arugula, and some
Pesto (see page 158), then add the sandwich tops
and serve.

prawn kebabs

Serves **4**

Preparation time **10 minutes**,
plus marinating

Cooking time **18–23 minutes**

12 **Dublin Bay prawn**,
thawed if frozen, peeled with
tails left on, deveined

¾ cup **long-grain rice**

1 cup frozen **peas**

8 **bacon slices**, rind removed,
halved lengthwise, and
rolled up

¼ cup **margarine** or **butter**

4 oz **mushrooms**, trimmed
and sliced

Balsamic marinade

5 tablespoons **olive oil**

2 tablespoons **balsamic
vinegar**

2 tablespoons chopped
oregano or **marjoram**

2 **garlic cloves**, crushed

black pepper

Mix all the marinade ingredients in a shallow bowl. Add the prawns to the marinade, turning to coat thoroughly. Cover and allow to marinate for 1 hour.

Put the rice in a large saucepan of boiling salted water and cook for 12–15 minutes or until just tender. Pour into a colander to drain.

Meanwhile, cook the peas in a separate saucepan of simmering salted water for about 5 minutes or until they are just tender. Drain the peas thoroughly.

Drain the prawns, reserving the marinade, and thread onto 4 metal skewers, alternating with the bacon rolls.

Cook on a hot barbecue for 6–8 minutes, turning the skewers several times and brushing the prawns and bacon with the remaining marinade, until the prawns are tender and cooked through and the bacon is crisp.

Meanwhile, melt the margarine in a saucepan, add the mushrooms and fry gently for about 3 minutes, until soft.

Stir the rice and peas into the pan and season to taste. Pile the rice mixture onto a heated serving dish and serve with the kebabs arranged on top.

For minted seafood kebabs, marinate 8 oz each of cubed angler fish and salmon in lime yogurt marinade (see page 186) for 30 minutes. Remove from the marinade and thread alternately onto soaked bamboo skewers. Cook on a medium-hot barbecue for 3–4 minutes on each side until cooked through. Serve with the vegetable rice as above.

chicken satay sticks

Serves **4**
Preparation time **10 minutes**,
  plus marinating
Cooking time **4–6 minutes**

4 skinless **chicken fillets**,
  about 4 oz each, sliced
  lengthwise into 3 strips
chopped **cilantro**, to garnish

Marinade
4 tablespoons **soy sauce**
4 tablespoons **lime juice**
1 **garlic clove**, crushed
1 teaspoon **curry powder**
1 teaspoon **peanut butter**
pinch of **dried red pepper
  flakes**

Satay sauce
1 tablespoon **peanut butter**
2 tablespoons **lime juice**
1 teaspoon **curry powder**
1 **garlic clove**, crushed
4 tablespoons **water**

Soak 12 bamboo skewers in cold water for
30 minutes. Put all the marinade ingredients
in a shallow dish and mix until smooth.

Thread the pieces of chicken onto the skewers.
Place in the dish of marinade, coat well, and allow
to marinate at room temperature for up to 2 hours.

Put all the sauce ingredients in a small bowl and mix
until smooth.

Cook the chicken sticks on a hot barbecue for
2–3 minutes on each side. Garnish with chopped
cilantro and serve with plenty of the satay sauce
for dipping.

For beef satay sticks, cut 1 lb beef tenderloin
into thin strips and thread onto 12 soaked skewers,
zigzagging back and forth as you go. Marinate in the
satay sauce as above, then cook on a hot barbecue
for 2–3 minutes on each side. Serve with Nam Jim
Dressing (see page 112)

seafood

moroccan salmon with fattoush

Serves **4**

Preparation time **20 minutes**, plus marinating

Cooking time **7–9 minutes**

4 **salmon fillets**, about 7 oz each

1 quantity **Moroccan Spice Paste** (see page 190)

spray oil

Fattoush salad

1 **green bell pepper**, seeded and diced

1 **Lebanese cucumber**, diced

2 ripe **tomatoes**, diced

½ **red onion**, finely chopped

2 tablespoons chopped **parsley**

2 tablespoons chopped **cilantro**

2 large **flatbreads**

3 tablespoons **extra virgin olive oil**

1 tablespoon **lemon juice**

salt and **black pepper**

Use tweezers to remove any small bones from the salmon fillets and place in a ceramic dish. Add the spice paste and rub all over the fish. Marinate for 2–4 hours.

Make the salad. Mix together the pepper, cucumber, tomatoes, and onion and herbs in a bowl. Toast the flatbreads on a hot barbecue for 30 seconds or so on each side, cool slightly, and tear into bite-size pieces. Add to the bowl with the olive oil and lemon juice. Season and stir well.

Remove the fish from its dish, spray with a little oil and cook on the hot barbecue for 3–4 minutes on each side until lightly charred and cooked to your liking. Rest briefly, then serve with the salad.

For salmon wrapped in prosciutto, wrap 4 x 7 oz skinless salmon fillets in a slice of prosciutto, securing in place with a toothpick. Cook the parcels on a hot barbecue for 3–4 minutes on each side, rest briefly, and serve with Salsa Rossa (see page 92).

red mullet & vine leaf parcels

Serves **4**
Preparation time **20 minutes**
Cooking time **8–10 minutes**

6 tablespoons **olive oil**
2 tablespoons **lemon juice**
2 tablespoons chopped **dill**
2 **scallions**, chopped
1 teaspoon **powdered mustard**
8 **vine leaves** in brine, drained
4 **red mullet**, about 12 oz each, scaled and gutted
4 **bay leaves**
4 **dill sprigs**, plus extra to garnish
salt and **black pepper**
lemon wedges, to garnish

Put 4 pieces of string, about 12 inches long, into cold water to soak for 10 minutes.

Put the oil, lemon juice, chopped dill, scallions, powdered mustard, and salt and pepper in a bowl and mix well. Wash and dry the vine leaves and arrange them in pairs, overlapping them slightly.

Make several slashes on both sides of each fish and rub them all over with a little of the oil and lemon mixture. Stuff each of the belly cavities with a bay leaf and a dill sprig. Lay each fish on a pair of vine leaves and wrap securely. Brush with a little of the oil and lemon mixture and fasten with the wet string to secure the leaves in place.

Cook the fish on a hot barbecue for 4–5 minutes on each side, brushing them with a little more of the oil and lemon mixture if necessary, until lightly charred. Allow the fish to rest for a few minutes, then discard the string and vine leaves and dress the mullet with the rest of the oil and lemon mixture. Garnish with dill sprigs and serve with a Tomato & Olive Salad (see page 86), if desired.

For goat cheese & vine leaf parcels, cut 8 oz goat cheese log into 8 thick slices. Place a slice in the middle of a large washed and dried vine leaf, wrap the leaf over and around the cheese slice, and secure with cooking string. Repeat to make 8 parcels. Cook on a hot barbecue for 2–3 minutes on each side until the cheese starts to ooze. Serve spread on slices of toasted French bread.

clam parcels with coconut

Serves **4**

Preparation time **10 minutes**,
plus soaking

Cooking time **8 minutes**

4 lb **fresh clams**

2 **garlic cloves**, chopped

2 teaspoons peeled and
grated **fresh ginger root**

1 large **red chili**, seeded and
finely chopped

8 **lime leaves**, torn

1 **lemon grass stalk**, bruised
and roughly chopped

¾ cup **coconut cream**

juice of 1 **lime**

1 tablespoon **light brown
sugar**

chopped **cilantro**, to garnish

crusty **bread**, to serve

Soak the clams in plenty of cold water for 1 hour, then drain, wash the clams and scrub the shells if they appear dirty. Arrange 4 large pieces of foil on a work surface and place a quarter of the clams in the center of each one. Top each one with a quarter of the garlic, ginger, chili, lime leaves, and lemon grass and draw the edges of the foil up to form "cups."

Combine the coconut cream, lime juice, and sugar and pour a quarter into each "cup." Seal the edges of the foil and cook the parcels on a hot barbecue for 8 minutes. Transfer the parcels to 4 plates, garnish with cilantro, and serve with crusty bread.

For clam parcels with garlic & chive butter, beat together ½ cup softened butter, 1 crushed garlic clove, 2 tablespoons snipped chives, and some black pepper. Divide the clams between foil "cups," following the method above, and add 2 tablespoons dry white wine to each one. Dot with the flavored butter, then seal the parcels. Cook as above and serve with crusty bread.

scallops with nam jim dressing

Serves **4**
Preparation time **5 minutes**
Cooking time **3 minutes**

24 **scallops on the half shell**
 or **shelled**

Nam jim dressing
1 large **red chili**, seeded and
 roughly chopped
1 **red birds eye chili**, seeded
 and roughly chopped
2 **garlic cloves**, chopped
pinch of **salt**
1 tablespoon chopped
 cilantro
2 tablespoons **palm sugar**,
 grated or **dark brown sugar**
1 tablespoon **Thai fish sauce**
2 tablespoons freshly
 squeezed **lime juice**

Start by making the dressing. Pound the chilies, garlic, and salt to form a rough paste using a mortar and pestle. Transfer to a bowl and stir in the cilantro, palm sugar, fish sauce, and lime juice, then stir until the sugar has dissolved.

Loosen the scallops from their shells with a small knife. Place the shells on a hot barbecue and cook for 3 minutes. Arrange the shells on plates and top each one with a spoonful of the dressing. Serve hot.

Alternatively, thread shelled scallops onto bamboo skewers that have been soaked in cold water for 30 minutes. Cook for 1 minute on each side and serve with the dressing.

For scallops with preserved lemon salsa, combine
½ diced preserved lemon, 10 diced semidried tomatoes, 2 finely chopped scallions, 1 tablespoon chopped basil, 4 tablespoons extra virgin olive oil and some salt and pepper. Cook the scallops following the above method and serve topped with the preserved lemon salsa.

chargrilled squid with chili jam

Serves **4**
Preparation time **15 minutes**,
    plus cooling and marinating
Cooking time **50 minutes**

2 lb cleaned **squid**
2–4 **garlic cloves**, crushed
1 tablespoon **sea salt**
1 tablespoon **light brown
    sugar**
lime wedges, to garnish

Chili jam
4 **birds eye chilies**
1 lb **tomatoes**
2 **garlic cloves**, crushed
¾ cup **light brown sugar**
½ cup **red wine vinegar**
salt and **black pepper**

Place all the chili jam ingredients in a saucepan, bring the mixture to a boil, and simmer for 45 minutes until thickened and jam-like. Allow to cool completely.

Remove the tentacles from inside the squid bodies and slice the tentacles away from the beak part of the head. Remove the quill from inside each body, if present.

Cut the bodies in half lengthwise and then again crosswise, then, using a sharp knife, score the inside with a diamond pattern. Place the squid pieces in a bowl. Add the garlic, salt, and sugar and rub in well, then allow to marinate for 15 minutes.

Cook the squid on a hot barbecue for 1–2 minutes, garnish with lime wedges, and serve with the chili jam.

For squid piri-piri, make some Piri-piri Sauce (see page 198). Take 8 medium-size squid bodies and cut in half lengthwise. Score the bodies as above, brush with oil, and season with salt and pepper. Cook on a hot barbecue for 1–2 minutes, then transfer to a board and cut into small pieces. Serve with the piri-piri sauce drizzled over.

shrimp with asian dressing

Serves **4**
Preparation time **10 minutes**,
  plus marinating
Cooking time **6 minutes**

24 raw peeled large **shrimp**,
  deveined

Marinade
4 tablespoons **olive oil**
2 **garlic cloves**, sliced
2 teaspoons peeled and
  grated **fresh ginger root**
1 **red birds eye chili**, seeded
  and sliced
4 **lime leaves**, torn
1 **lemon grass stalk**, finely
  sliced
2 tablespoons **Thai fish
  sauce**
2 tablespoons **lime juice**
4 teaspoons **light brown
  sugar**
salt and **black pepper**

To garnish
1 tablespoon each chopped
  cilantro, mint, and **Thai
  basil leaves**
1 large **red chili**, seeded and
  sliced

Combine the marinade ingredients in a nonmetallic
dish. Add the shrimp and stir well, then allow to
marinate for 30 minutes. Meanwhile, soak 24 bamboo
skewers in cold water for 30 minutes.

Thread one shrimp onto each skewer and tip the
marinade juices into a small pan.

Cook the shrimp on a hot barbecue for 2 minutes
on each side, then arrange on a platter. Heat the pan
juices until they come to a boil, then pour over the
shrimp. Serve garnished with the herbs and chili slices.

For Asian mixed-leaf salad, to serve as an
accompaniment, place 2½ cups mixed Asian leaves
in a bowl. Add 1 finely grated carrot, ½ seeded and
finely sliced cucumber, and 1 cup bean sprouts. Beat
2 tablespoons extra virgin olive oil with 2 teaspoons
light soy sauce, 1 teaspoon lime juice, and 1 teaspoon
honey, add the dressing to the salad and toss well.

sea bass with lime aïoli

Serves **4**
Preparation time **30 minutes**
Cooking time **20–25 minutes**

4 large **potatoes**, scrubbed
4 tablespoons **olive oil**
4 **sea bass fillets**, 6–8 oz
  each
salt and **black pepper**

Lime aïoli
4–6 **garlic cloves**, crushed
2 **egg yolks**
juice and finely grated zest of
  2 **limes**
1¼ cups **extra virgin olive oil**

To garnish
grilled **lime slices**
snipped **chives**

Make the aïoli by placing the garlic and egg yolks in a food processor or blender, adding the lime juice, and processing briefly to mix. With the machine running, gradually add the olive oil in a thin, steady stream until the mixture forms a thick cream. Turn into a bowl, stir in the lime zest, and season with salt and pepper. Set aside.

Slice the potatoes thinly and brush well with olive oil. Sprinkle the slices with salt and pepper and cook on a hot barbecue for 8–10 minutes on each side or until tender and golden. Remove from the heat and keep warm.

Score the sea bass fillets, brush well with the remaining olive oil and cook, skin side down, on the barbecue for 3–4 minutes until just cooked, turning once. Remove from the heat and serve the fish, potatoes, and aïoli garnished with lime slices and snipped chives.

For soy & ginger sea bass parcels, place 4 x 7 oz sea bass fillets in the center of 4 large squares of foil. Top each with a little sliced scallion, some shredded ginger, a slice of garlic, and a star anise. Combine 1 tablespoon dark soy sauce with the juice of ½ lime, 2 tablespoons rice wine (or dry sherry), and 2 teaspoons sesame oil and divide between the fish portions. Wrap up to form parcels and cook on a hot barbecue for 5 minutes. Remove and allow to rest for 5 minutes, then serve with steamed rice.

blackened tuna with mango salsa

Serves **4**
Preparation time **10 minutes**,
  plus marinating
Cooking time **2 minutes**

4 **tuna steaks**, about 8 oz
  each
1 tablespoon **extra virgin
  olive oil**
2 tablespoons freshly crushed
  black pepper
1 teaspoon **salt**
lime slices, to garnish

Mango salsa
1 large **mango**, about 1 lb,
  diced
½ **red onion**, finely chopped
1 large **red chili**, seeded and
  finely chopped
1 tablespoon **lime juice**
2 tablespoons chopped
  cilantro
salt and **black pepper**

Make the mango salsa by combining all the ingredients in a bowl and seasoning to taste. Set aside for the flavors to develop.

Brush the tuna steaks with a little oil and season with the peppercorns and salt. Cook the tuna on a hot barbecue for about 1 minute on each side (or a little less if wished). Rest briefly, then serve with the salsa and the lime slices to garnish.

For open-grilled tuna burger, chargrill 4 seasoned tuna steaks, about 8 oz each, following the method above, drizzle with lemon juice, and allow to rest briefly. Toast 4 bread slices on the barbecue for 1 minute on each side until charred. Remove, then rub with peeled garlic and drizzle with extra virgin olive oil. Top each toast with a tuna steak and the juices and serve topped with arugula leaves, sliced tomatoes, and some Aïoli (see page 122).

salt-rubbed shrimp with aïoli

Serves **4**
Preparation time **10 minutes**
Cooking time **4–6 minutes**

24 raw **jumbo shrimp**
2 tablespoons **extra virgin
  olive oil**
2 tablespoons **sea salt**

Aïoli
3 **egg yolks**
2 teaspoons **white wine
  vinegar**
1 teaspoon **Dijon mustard**
2–4 **garlic cloves**, crushed
1¼ cups **olive oil**
salt and **white pepper**

Place the shrimp in a large bowl, add the oil and salt, and toss well together so the shrimp are lightly coated with the salt.

Make the aïoli. Place the egg yolks, vinegar, mustard, garlic cloves, and a little salt and pepper in a food processor and blend briefly until the egg mixture is frothy. Then, with the blade running, gradually pour in the oil through the funnel until the sauce is thickened and glossy. Thin with a little boiling water if the sauce is too thick. Adjust the seasoning to taste.

Cook the shrimp on a hot barbecue for 2–3 minutes on each side. Serve with the aïoli to dip the shrimp into once they've been peeled, and an arugula salad.

For chargrilled shrimp with chili & garlic butter,
peel and devein 24 large shrimp and thread onto presoaked bamboo skewers. Spray with a little oil and barbecue on a high heat for 3–4 minutes until evenly charred and cooked through. Squeeze over a little lemon juice. Meanwhile, place 1 seeded and chopped large red chili, 2 crushed garlic cloves, and ½ cup butter in a saucepan and heat gently until melted and the garlic is softened, about 3 minutes. Serve the butter as a sauce for the shrimp.

swordfish with walnuts & beans

Serves **4**
Preparation time **15 minutes**
Cooking time **6 minutes**

4 **swordfish steaks**, about
   7 oz each
extra virgin olive oil, for
   brushing
2 tablespoons **balsamic glaze**
salt and **black pepper**

Salad
8 oz **fine green beans**,
   trimmed
8 oz **yellow beans**, trimmed
½ cup **walnuts**, toasted
2 tablespoons torn **parsley**
   leaves
2 tablespoons torn **mint**
   leaves

Dressing
3 tablespoons **walnut oil**
1 tablespoon **extra virgin**
   olive oil
1 tablespoon **sherry vinegar**
1 teaspoon **superfine sugar**
1 small **garlic clove**, crushed

Rub the swordfish steaks with oil and season with salt and pepper.

Make the salad. Cook the beans in a saucepan of lightly salted boiling water for 3 minutes, drain well, and refresh under cold water. Pat dry. Place in a bowl and add the walnuts and herbs and a little salt and pepper.

Beat the dressing ingredients together in a bowl and season with salt and pepper. Drizzle over the salad and toss well.

Cook the swordfish steaks on a hot barbecue for 1–1½ minutes on each side. Wrap loosely in foil and set aside to rest for 3 minutes. Arrange the swordfish on plates, drizzle with the balsamic glaze, and serve with the bean salad.

For homemade balsamic glaze, pour 2 cups cheap balsamic vinegar into a saucepan and bring to a boil. Simmer fast for 10–15 minutes until the vinegar is reduced to about ½ cup. Set aside to cool. Store in a clean bottle and use as required.

buttery lobster tails with aïoli

Serves **4**
Preparation time **20 minutes**
Cooking time **14–16 minutes**

4 raw **lobster tails**
¼ cup **butter**
2 tablespoons **ready-made**
   or **homemade garlic &**
   saffron oil (see below)
1 tablespoon snipped **chives**
½ recipe quantity **Aïoli**
   (see page 122), with
   ½ tablespoon **lemon juice**
   added with the eggs
cucumber ribbons, made
   using a vegetable peeler

To garnish
finely grated zest of **1 lemon**
2 tablespoons chopped
   chervil

Dot the lobster tails with the butter and drizzle with the garlic and saffron oil. Cook the lobster tails on a hot barbecue for 7–8 minutes each side, or until cooked through.

Stir the chives into the aïoli. Sprinkle the lobster with the lemon zest and chopped chervil and serve immediately with the cucumber ribbons and aïoli in small bowls.

For homemade garlic & saffron oil, which is also perfect for making quick and interesting Italian bruschettas, heat 2 cups extra virgin olive oil very gently in a saucepan with 10–12 garlic cloves and 1 teaspoon saffron threads. (The idea is just to warm the oil, not to get it hot.) Remove the pan from the heat and let it cool completely, then pour the oil and the flavorings into a clean bottle and stopper tightly. Leave in a cool place for 2 weeks, then either use immediately or strain to prevent harmful bacteria from growing in it, then pour into a clean bottle and keep for up to 6 months.

olive & citrus salmon

Serves **4**

Preparation time **5 minutes**

Cooking time **8–10 minutes**

4 **salmon fillets**, about 7 oz
 each

12 large **black olives**, pitted
 and halved

12 **cherry tomatoes**, halved

4 tablespoons **extra virgin
 olive oil**

2 wedges **preserved lemon**,
 thinly sliced

2 teaspoons **honey**

salt and **black pepper**

chopped **parsley**, to garnish

Use tweezers to remove any small bones from the salmon fillets. Place on 4 large pieces of foil and top each with a quarter of the olives, tomatoes, oil, preserved lemon, and honey. Season with salt and pepper and seal the parcels well.

Cook the parcels on a hot barbecue for 8–10 minutes, then remove from the heat and rest briefly. Carefully open the parcels, garnish with chopped parsley, and serve with a Couscous Salad (see page 156).

For foil-wrapped cod with soy, ginger, & sesame, place 4 cod fillets on foil, as above, drawing the edges up slightly to form "cups." Add 1 tablespoon dry sherry, 1 tablespoon dark soy sauce, a little shredded fresh ginger root, a little sliced garlic, and 1 teaspoon sesame oil to each one. Seal the foil and cook as above. Serve with plain boiled rice.

juniper & peppercorn salmon

Serves **6**

Preparation time **10 minutes,**
  plus marinating

Cooking time **8–10 minutes**

6 **salmon fillets,** about 7 oz
  each
frisée lettuce leaves, to serve

**Juniper & peppercorn
marinade**
1½ tablespoons **dried juniper
  berries**
2 teaspoons **dried green
  peppercorns**
¼ teaspoon **black
  peppercorns**
1 teaspoon **Demerara sugar**
2–3 tablespoons **oil**

To garnish
lemon wedges
parsley sprigs
2 **scallions,** finely shredded

Make the marinade by coarsely grinding the juniper berries and peppercorns in a spice grinder or using a mortar and pestle. Mix with the sugar and oil.

Use tweezers to remove any small bones from the salmon fillets. Brush the fillets with the marinade and allow to marinate at room temperature for 1 hour.

Wrap each salmon fillet in a piece of foil, sealing the edges well. Cook on a hot barbecue for 8–10 minutes, then set aside to rest briefly. Unwrap the salmon, garnish with lemon wedges, parsley sprigs, and scallions and serve with frisée lettuce leaves.

For pork tenderloin with juniper & peppercorns,

make the marinade as above and place in a shallow dish. Trim 4 x 7 oz pork tenderloins and coat with the marinade. Cover and chill for 2 hours. Remove the pork and cook on a medium-hot barbecue for 12–15 minutes until evenly browned. Allow to rest for 5 minutes, then serve with Spinach Salad (see page 60).

mackerel with citrus fennel salad

Serves **4**

Preparation time **10 minutes**

Cooking time **8–10 minutes**

4 **mackerel**, about 13 oz each
spray oil

3 **lemons**, thinly sliced, plus
　2 tablespoons lemon juice

1 **fennel bulb**, trimmed and
　thinly sliced, fronds reserved

1 small **garlic clove**, crushed

2 tablespoons drained **capers**

2 tablespoons **extra virgin
　olive oil**

1 tablespoon chopped
　parsley

salt and **black pepper**

Slash each mackerel 3–4 times on each side with a sharp knife. Spray with a little oil and season inside and out with salt and pepper. Using cooking string, tie 3 lemon slices on each side of the fish. Spray with a little oil and cook on a hot barbecue for 4–5 minutes on each side until lightly charred and cooked through. Set aside to rest for 5 minutes.

Place the fennel in a bowl with the garlic, capers, oil, parsley, fennel fronds, and lemon juice and season to taste. Serve the mackerel with the fennel salad.

For chargrilled sardines with salsa verde, prepare 20 medium sardines following the method above and cook on a hot barbecue for 3–4 minutes on each side. Squeeze with lemon juice and serve the sardines with Salsa Verde (see page 48).

vegetarian
dishes

corn with chili salt

Serves **6**
Preparation time **5 minutes**
Cooking time **25 minutes**

6 **corn ears**, husked and
  trimmed
2 tablespoons **sea salt**
½ teaspoon **dried red pepper
  flakes**
5 tablespoons **butter**
1 **lime**, cut into wedges,
  to garnish

Blanch the corn in a large saucepan in 2 separate batches for 10 minutes. Drain well and pat dry on paper towels. Cook the ears on a hot barbecue for 5–6 minutes, turning frequently, until evenly charred and tender.

Meanwhile, place the salt and pepper flakes in a mortar and pound with a pestle until the salt turns a rusty red.

Place the corn on plates and top with butter, sprinkle with the salt mixture, and garnish with the lime wedges.

For smoky corn salsa, follow the recipe above to cook and barbecue 1 corn ear, then, using a sharp knife, cut down the ear to remove the kernels. Place in a bowl and, when cool, stir in 2 finely chopped scallions, 1 seeded and chopped tomato, 1 seeded and finely chopped large red chili, 1 crushed garlic clove, juice of ½ lime, 2 tablespoons chopped cilantro, and some salt and pepper.

mustard & thyme sweet potatoes

Serves **6**
Preparation time **5 minutes**
Cooking time **40 minutes**

6 **sweet potatoes**, about
    8 oz each, scrubbed

Mustard & thyme butter
½ cup **butter**, softened
1 tablespoon **wholegrain
    mustard**
1 teaspoon chopped **thyme**
black pepper

Wrap each potato in a double layer of foil and either place them on the flat plate of a gas barbecue or, using barbecue tongs, set them in among the heated coals of a charcoal barbecue, allowing some of the coals to cover the potatoes. Bake for 40 minutes.

Meanwhile, make the butter. Place the butter, mustard, thyme, and some pepper in a bowl and mash with a fork until evenly mixed. Set aside.

Remove the potatoes from the barbecue (again using tongs) and carefully remove the foil using oven mitts. Cut the potatoes in half and serve topped with the butter.

For classic sweet potato wedges, cut 4 small sweet potatoes into wedges and brush with a little oil. Season with salt and pepper and cook over a medium heat for 30 minutes, turning halfway through until charred and cooked through. Sprinkle with some sea salt to serve.

spinach & sweet potato cakes

Serves **4**

Preparation time **35 minutes**,
  plus infusing

Cooking time **40 minutes**

1 lb **sweet potatoes**, cut into
  chunks

2½ cups **spinach leaves**

4–5 **scallions**, sliced

1 cup **snow peas**, finely
  shredded

½ cup **corn kernels**

⅓ cup pitted **black olives**,
  finely chopped

3 tablespoons **sesame seeds**

4 tablespoons **flour**

olive oil, for brushing

salt and **black pepper**

Chili & coconut dip

¾ cup **coconut cream**

2 **red chilies**, seeded and
  finely chopped

1 **lemon grass stalk**, sliced

3 **kaffir lime leaves**, shredded

bunch of **cilantro**, chopped

1 tablespoon **light soy sauce**

2 tablespoons **sesame oil**

To garnish

lime wedges

scallions, shredded

Bring a large saucepan of salted water to a boil, add
the sweet potatoes and cook for about 20 minutes
until tender. Drain the potatoes, then return them to the
pan and place over a low heat for 1 minute, stirring
constantly to evaporate any excess moisture. Lightly
mash the potatoes with a fork.

Meanwhile, put the spinach leaves in a colander and
pour a pan of boiling water over. Rinse the spinach with
cold water and squeeze the leaves dry. Stir the wilted
spinach into the potatoes, then add the scallions, snow
peas, corn, and olives. Season well with salt and pepper
and set aside to cool.

Make the dip. Gently warm the coconut cream in a
small saucepan with the chilies, lemon grass, and lime
leaves for about 10 minutes, without letting it reach
boiling point. Set aside to infuse.

Use your hands to form the potato mixture into
12 little cakes. Mix the sesame seeds and flour
together and sprinkle the mixture over the cakes.
Brush the cakes with a little oil, then cook on a
moderately hot barbecue for 4–5 minutes. Once
a crisp crust has formed, turn them over and cook
for an additional 4–5 minutes on the other side.

Stir the cilantro, soy sauce, and sesame oil into the
dip and pour it into individual dishes. Serve immediately
with the potato cakes, garnished with lime wedges
and shredded scallions.

bruschetta with charred fennel

Serves **4**
Preparation time **10 minutes**
Cooking time **17 minutes**

2 large **fennel bulbs**, about
    13 oz total weight, trimmed
    and fronds reserved
3 tablespoons **extra virgin
    olive oil**
4 oz **feta cheese**, diced
½ cup pitted **black olives**,
    halved
2 tablespoons chopped
    parsley
squeeze of **lemon juice**
4 slices of **sourdough bread**
2 **garlic cloves**
1¼ cups **wild arugula leaves**
salt and **black pepper**

Cut the fennel bulbs lengthwise into ¼ inch thick slices and place in a large bowl. Add 1 tablespoon of the oil and toss well. Cook on a hot barbecue for 15 minutes, turning halfway through, until charred and tender.

Transfer the fennel to a bowl and add the feta, olives, parsley, lemon juice, and some salt and pepper and toss well.

Toast the bread slices on the barbecue for 1 minute on each side until browned. Rub the charred bread on both sides with the garlic cloves and drizzle with a little of the remaining oil. Top with the fennel salad and arugula and serve drizzled with the remaining oil.

For bruschetta with grilled peppers, cut 2 large red bell peppers into quarters and discard the seeds. Brush with a little oil and chargrill for 2–3 minutes on each side until tender. Cool in a plastic bag, then peel and discard the skin and cut the flesh into slices. Combine the peppers with 2 tablespoons extra virgin olive oil, 2 teaspoons balsamic vinegar, 1 crushed garlic clove, 6 quartered cherry tomatoes, a few torn basil leaves, and some salt and pepper. Chargrill 4 ciabatta slices following the above recipe and serve topped with the pepper mixture.

tomato, pesto, & olive pizza

Serves **2**

Preparation time **15 minutes**, plus rising

Cooking time **20–24 minutes**

spray oil

2 tablespoons **Pesto** (see page 158)

7 oz **cherry tomatoes**, halved

5 oz **mozzarella cheese**, sliced

⅓ cup pitted **black olives**, halved

handful of **basil leaves**

salt and **black pepper**

Pizza dough

2 cups **white bread flour**

½ teaspoon **salt**

1 teaspoon **active dry yeast**

½ cup warm **water**

1 tablespoon **extra virgin olive oil**, plus extra to drizzle

Make the pizza dough. Sift the flour into a bowl and stir in the salt and yeast. Make a well in the middle and gradually work in the measured water and the oil until the mixture comes together in a ball. Transfer to a lightly floured surface and knead for 8–10 minutes or until the dough is smooth. Place in an oiled bowl, cover with plastic wrap, and allow to rise for 1 hour until doubled in size.

Knock the air from the dough and cut in half. Roll one piece out on a floured surface to form a 9 inch round. Lightly spray a heavy skillet with oil and press the dough into the base. Spread half the pesto over the dough and top with half the tomatoes, mozzarella, and olives, some salt and pepper and a drizzle more oil.

Place the pan on a moderately hot barbecue, cover with the barbecue lid or a wok lid and cook for 10–12 minutes until the dough is crisp underneath and the cheese melted. Carefully slide the pizza out onto a board, garnish with half the basil leaves, and serve hot. Make the second pizza.

For garlic & rosemary pizza, follow the recipe above to make the pizza dough and roll out to the required size. Combine 2 crushed garlic cloves, 1 tablespoon chopped rosemary, some salt and pepper, and 4 tablespoons extra virgin olive oil. Cook the pizza bases following the method above, but this time turn halfway through with a spatula, so that both sides brown. Remove from the heat and brush each one with the garlic and rosemary oil. Serve hot.

sesame-lime buttered corn

Serves **6**
Preparation time **15 minutes,**
    plus chilling
Cooking time **25–30 minutes**

1 tablespoon **sesame seeds**
4 tablespoons **unsalted**
    butter, softened
1 small **red chili,** seeded and
    finely chopped
grated zest and juice of
    ½–1 **lime,** plus extra zest
    to garnish
3 small **corn ears**
salt and **black pepper**
watercress, to garnish

Dry-fry the sesame seeds in a small skillet until golden. Allow to cool slightly, then place in a food processor or blender with the butter, chili, lime zest and juice, and salt and pepper to taste and blend until combined. Transfer the butter to a piece of foil and roll into a sausage shape. Chill for 30 minutes, then remove from the foil and cut into thin slices.

Parboil the corn ears for 5 minutes, then cut into ½ inch slices. Place on double-thickness pieces of foil, top with the butter slices, and wrap up the foil parcels tightly. Cook on a hot barbecue for 20–25 minutes until the corn is tender. Garnish with lime zest and some watercress and serve immediately with more butter slices.

For cilantro & chili butter, instead of the sesame-lime butter, combine ½ cup softened butter with 2 tablespoons chopped fresh cilantro, 1 seeded and finely chopped red chili, and some black pepper. Mash well and wrap and chill as above. Serve in slices with barbecued foods.

potato skins & sour cream dip

Serves **6**
Preparation time **8 minutes**
Cooking time **4 minutes**

6 large **potatoes**, baked and
   allowed to go cold
1⅓ cups grated **cheddar
   cheese**
spray oil

Dip
¾ cup **sour cream**
1 **garlic clove**, crushed
1 tablespoon chopped **chives**
salt and **black pepper**

Take the cooled potatoes and cut into quarters. Scoop out and discard the potato flesh (or use for another recipe). Transfer the skins to a bowl and spray with a little oil.

Cook the skins cut-side down on the barbecue for 2 minutes, turn, and carefully sprinkle a little cheese onto each skin. Cook for an additional 2 minutes until the cheese is melted.

Meanwhile, make the dip. Combine the ingredients in a bowl and season to taste. Serve the skins with the dipping sauce.

For new potato skewers, parboil 20 small new potatoes for 10 minutes, drain and refresh under cold water. Pat dry and thread the potatoes onto 4 presoaked bamboo skewers. Spray with a little oil and cook on a hot barbecue for 5–6 minutes on each side until the potatoes are charred and cooked through. Serve with Aïoli (see page 122).

moroccan carrot salad

Serves **4–6**
Preparation time **10 minutes**
Cooking time **15–20 minutes**

2 bunches of **carrots**, trimmed
spray oil
3 tablespoons **sunflower
 seeds**, toasted
2 tablespoons chopped
 parsley

Dressing
4 tablespoons **extra virgin
 olive oil**
2 tablespoons **white wine
 vinegar**
1 **garlic clove**, finely chopped
1 teaspoon **pomegranate
 syrup**
1 teaspoon **honey**
salt and **black pepper**

Blanch the carrots in a large pan of lightly salted boiling water for 10 minutes. Drain well and pat dry. Transfer to a bowl and spray with a little oil, then cook on a hot barbecue for 5–10 minutes, turning frequently, until charred.

Meanwhile, combine the dressing ingredients in a large bowl and season to taste. Stir in the cooked carrots, sunflower seeds, and parsley and toss well. Serve hot.

For grilled carrots with mustard & chive butter, follow the above recipe to cook the carrots. Meanwhile, beat ¼ cup softened butter with 2 teaspoons wholegrain mustard, 1 tablespoon snipped chives, and a little pepper. Toss the cooked carrots with the butter until coated and serve hot.

vegetable kebabs with tabbouleh

Serves **4**
Preparation time **15 minutes**,
  plus marinating
Cooking time **10–15 minutes**

1 tablespoon chopped
  rosemary
2 **zucchini**, thickly sliced
1 large **red bell pepper**,
  seeded and quartered
16 **button mushrooms**,
  trimmed
16 large **cherry tomatoes**
ready-made or **homemade**
  tzatziki (see below), to serve

Tabbouleh
1½ cups **bulghur wheat**
4 tablespoons each chopped
  cilantro, parsley, and **mint**
2 **tomatoes**, diced
⅔ cup **extra virgin olive oil**
3 tablespoons **red wine**
  vinegar
salt and **pepper**

Put the bulghur wheat in a bowl, pour enough water over to cover the wheat by 2 inches and allow to soak for 20 minutes. Drain well, then stir in the cilantro, mint, parsley, tomatoes, ½ cup of the oil, vinegar, and salt and pepper.

Meanwhile, in a large bowl combine the rosemary with the remaining oil and some salt and pepper. Add the zucchini, pepper, mushrooms, and cherry tomatoes to the oil, toss well, and marinate for 15 minutes. Thread onto metal skewers.

Cook the kebabs on a hot barbecue for 10–15 minutes, turning halfway through, until all the vegetables are cooked. Serve with the tabbouleh and some tzatziki.

For homemade tzatziki, finely grate 1 cucumber and squeeze out as much water as possible. Stir into ¾ cup Greek-style or whole milk yogurt with 1 crushed garlic clove, 1 tablespoon chopped mint, and a little salt and pepper.

mushroom burgers with onion jam

Serves **4**
Preparation time **5 minutes**,
  plus cooling
Cooking time **30–40 minutes**

8 large **flat mushrooms**,
  trimmed
1 tablespoon **extra virgin
  olive oil**
4 **ciabatta rolls**
1 cup **baby spinach leaves**
salt and **black pepper**
Aïoli (see page 122), to serve
  (optional)

Onion jam
4 tablespoons **extra virgin
  olive oil**
4 **onions**, thinly sliced
4 **thyme sprigs**, lightly
  bruised
½ cup **light brown sugar**
6 tablespoons **red wine
  vinegar**
4 tablespoons **red currant
  jelly**

Make the onion jam. Heat the oil in a saucepan and gently fry the onions, thyme sprigs, and some salt and pepper for 20–25 minutes until really soft and golden. Discard the thyme sprigs and stir in the sugar, vinegar, and red currant jelly. Simmer for 6–8 minutes until the sauce is thick and jam-like, then allow to cool completely.

Brush the mushrooms with the oil and season with salt and pepper. Cook on a hot barbecue for 2–3 minutes on each side. Meanwhile, toast the ciabatta rolls for about 1 minute on each side until lightly browned.

Fill each roll with two mushrooms and some spinach leaves and spoon in some onion jam and aïoli, if desired. Serve at once.

For garlic mushroom parcels, trim 1 lb button mushrooms and divide between 4 large sheets of foil. Top each pile of mushrooms with 2 tablespoons butter, a little crushed garlic, a thyme sprig, and some salt and black pepper. Wrap the foil around the mushrooms to seal well and cook on a hot barbecue for 10–12 minutes. Carefully open the parcels and garnish with a little chopped parsley and a squeeze of lemon juice.

chili squash with couscous salad

Serves **4–6**
Preparation time **15 minutes**
Cooking time **20 minutes**

1 small **butternut squash,**
  about 2 lb
2 tablespoons **extra virgin**
  olive oil
1 tablespoon **balsamic**
  vinegar
1 teaspoon **hot chili sauce**
1 teaspoon **honey**
salt and **black pepper**

Couscous salad
1½ cups **couscous**
1 cup hot **vegetable stock**
4 **scallions,** finely chopped
2 tablespoons chopped
  preserved lemon
⅓ cup **raisins**
⅓ cup **pine nuts,** toasted
4 tablespoons chopped
  herbs, such as **cilantro,**
  mint, and **parsley**
juice of ½ **lemon**

Cut the squash in half and scoop out and discard the seeds, then cut crosswise into ½ inch thick slices. Place in a large bowl with half the oil and some salt and pepper and stir well to coat the squash. Cook on a medium barbecue for about 10 minutes on each side until charred and tender. Return to the bowl and add the remaining oil, balsamic vinegar, chili sauce, and honey and stir well.

Meanwhile, make the salad. Place the couscous in a bowl and pour over the stock. Allow to soak for 10 minutes, then fluff up the grains with a fork. Stir in the remaining ingredients and season to taste. Serve the couscous salad with the squash.

For grilled squash, onion, & feta salad, follow the method above to cook the squash. Cut 1 red onion into thick wedges, brush with a little olive oil, and barbecue for 3–4 minutes on each side until charred and tender. Place the squash and onion in a bowl, add 2½ cups arugula leaves, 4 oz diced feta cheese, ¼ cup toasted walnut pieces, 2 tablespoons walnut oil, 2 teaspoons sherry vinegar, and some salt and pepper, toss well and serve.

mediterranean burgers with pesto

Serves **4**
Preparation time **15 minutes**
Cooking time **4–6 minutes**

1 **eggplant**, cut into long
    strips about ⅛ inch thick
2 **zucchini**, cut into long strips
    about ⅛ inch thick
3 tablespoons **extra virgin
    olive oil**
4 **ciabatta rolls**, halved
2 **tomatoes**, sliced
5 oz **buffalo mozzarella
    cheese**, sliced
2½ cups **arugula leaves**

Pesto
1 cup **basil**
1 **garlic clove**, crushed
2 tablespoons **pine nuts**,
    toasted
¼ teaspoon **sea salt**
6–8 tablespoons **extra virgin
    olive oil**
2 tablespoons freshly grated
    Parmesan cheese
black pepper

Make the pesto. Place the basil, garlic, pine nuts, and sea salt in a mortar and grind with a pestle to form a fairly smooth paste. Slowly add the oil until you reach the required texture (soft but not runny), then finally add the cheese and pepper, to taste.

Brush the eggplant and zucchini strips with the oil and season with salt and pepper. Cook on a hot barbecue for 2–3 minutes on each side until charred and tender.

Spread the rolls with some pesto, then fill with the grilled vegetables, tomatoes, mozzarella, and arugula. Add a little extra pesto and serve hot.

For mayonnaise, instead of the pesto, place 3 egg yolks, 2 teaspoons white wine vinegar, 1 teaspoon Dijon mustard, and a little salt and pepper in a bowl and, using an electric beater, beat until the mixture is frothy. Then very gradually beat in 1¼ cups olive oil, a little at a time, beating well after each addition until the sauce is thickened and glossy and all the oil incorporated. Thin the sauce with a little boiling water, if too thick. Use as required or cover the surface with plastic wrap and refrigerate for up to 3 days.

salads, sauces, & marinades

mixed leaf & zucchini salad

Serves **4**
Preparation time **10 minutes**
Cooking time **10 minutes**

4 **zucchini**, cut into thick
  slices
olive oil, for brushing
2½ cups **mixed salad leaves**
handful of **mint leaves**, torn

Dressing
3 tablespoons **pine nuts**
4 tablespoons **extra virgin**
  olive oil
2 teaspoons **lemon juice**
1 teaspoon **honey**
salt and **black pepper**

Brush the zucchini slices with a little oil, then season. Cook on a hot barbecue for 2–3 minutes on each side, then set aside to cool. When cool, place in a bowl with the salad leaves and mint and stir well.

Make the dressing. Place the nuts in a skillet and heat until golden, shaking the pan so they cook evenly. Transfer to a mortar and bash lightly with a pestle until "smashed." Transfer to a bowl and beat in the oil, lemon juice, honey, and some salt and pepper to taste. Add to the salad and toss before serving.

For mixed leaf salad with bacon & croutons, dice 8 oz smoked bacon. Heat a skillet until hot, add the bacon and stir-fry for 3–4 minutes until crisp and the fat is released. Remove the bacon with a slotted spoon and set aside. Add 2 tablespoons extra virgin olive oil to the pan and gently fry 4 oz cubed bread for 4–5 minutes until crisp. Drain on paper towels. Place the bacon, bread, and 2½ cups mixed salad leaves in a bowl, drizzle over a little more oil, 1–2 teaspoons white wine vinegar, and some salt and black pepper. Toss well and serve.

pear & pecorino salad

Serves **4**
Preparation time **10 minutes**
Cooking time **2–4 minutes**

4 **pears**, peeled
5 cups **arugula**
4 tablespoons **olive oil**
2 tablespoons **balsamic
  vinegar**
5 oz **pecorino cheese**
salt and **black pepper**

Quarter and core the pears, then slice each quarter in half. Thread onto metal skewers, then place on a hot barbecue and cook for 1–2 minutes on each side.

Place the arugula in a bowl with the olive oil, balsamic vinegar, and a little salt and pepper and toss well.

Peel the pecorino into long ribbons using a vegetable peeler and add to the arugula. Arrange the mixture on 4 individual plates and place the barbecued pears on top. Serve immediately.

For bruschetta with pear & pecorino salad, brush 4 thick slices of sourdough bread with extra virgin olive oil. Toast on a hot barbecue for 1 minute on each side, then rub all over with a peeled garlic clove. Make the salad as above and spoon onto the bruschetta, drizzling a little more oil over the top.

tuna tataki salad & asian dressing

Serves **4**
Preparation time **10 minutes**
Cooking time **3 minutes**

4 tuna loin fillets or **steaks,**
about 7 oz each (note that
the tuna must be very fresh
as it is partly raw when
eaten)
2 teaspoons **sesame oil**
8 oz thin **asparagus**, trimmed
2 cups **mixed salad leaves**
salt and **black pepper**

**Sesame, soy, & ginger
dressing**
1 tablespoon **sunflower oil**
1 tablespoon **cold water**
4 teaspoons **rice wine
    vinegar**
1 tablespoon **soy sauce**
1½ teaspoons **superfine
    sugar**
1 teaspoon peeled and grated
fresh ginger root
1 teaspoon **sesame oil**

Brush the tuna with sesame oil and season well
with salt and pepper. Cook on a hot barbecue for
10 seconds on each side, then rinse under cold water
to stop the fish cooking more. Pat dry and set aside.

Stir the dressing ingredients together in a bowl and
season to taste.

Blanch the asparagus in lightly salted boiling water
for 2 minutes. Drain well, refresh under cold water,
and pat dry.

Arrange the salad leaves and asparagus on a large
platter. Slice the tuna thinly and arrange with the salad.
Drizzle with the dressing and serve.

For seared tuna with chili jam, lightly season
4 x 7 oz tuna steaks, brush with oil, and cook on a
hot barbecue for 1 minute on each side. Rest briefly,
then serve with Chili Jam (see page 114).

mushroom & watercress salad

Serves **4**
Preparation time **10 minutes**
Cooking time **22 minutes**

4 slices of **rustic bread**
4 large **flat mushrooms**,
    trimmed
4 oz **soft goat cheese**
3 tablespoons **olive oil**
1 tablespoon **cider vinegar**
2½ cups **watercress**
sea salt and **mixed**
    peppercorns, crushed

Toast the bread slices on a medium barbecue for 1 minute on each side until browned. Set aside, keeping warm.

Place the mushrooms on the barbecue, gills down, and cook for 10 minutes. Turn the mushrooms over and cook for another 10 minutes. (The undersides are cooked first to seal in all the juices.)

Place the toasted bread on 4 plates and spread each slice with some goat cheese. Mix together the olive oil, vinegar, and seasoning in a small bowl to make a dressing.

Remove the cooked mushrooms from the barbecue and slice. Mix them with the watercress and dressing and heap onto the toasted bread. Serve immediately.

For grilled mushrooms with lemon & thyme butter, beat 2 tablespoons chopped fresh thyme and the grated zest of 1 lemon into ½ cup butter with a little pepper. Trim 8 large flat mushrooms, spray with olive oil and cook, stem side up, on a medium-hot barbecue for 2–3 minutes. Turn over and dot with the butter, then grill for an additional 3–4 minutes until the mushrooms are tender. Serve with 4 slices of toasted bread.

root vegetable & arugula salad

Serves **4**
Preparation time **15 minutes**
Cooking time **40–55 minutes**

1 bunch of small **beets**, trimmed
1 bunch of **carrots**, trimmed
1 **red onion**, cut into thick wedges
spray oil
2½ cups **baby arugula**
1 cup **pecan nuts**, toasted

Dressing
4 oz **soft goat cheese**
4 teaspoons **white wine vinegar**
2 teaspoons **honey**
½ cup **extra virgin olive oil**, plus extra for brushing
2–3 tablespoons boiling **water**
salt and **black pepper**

Place the beets in a pan of cold water, bring to a boil and simmer for 20–30 minutes, then remove with a slotted spoon. Add the carrots to the pan and cook for 5 minutes. Cut the beets into wedges and thread onto 2 metal skewers.

Spray the beets and carrots with a little oil and cook on a hot barbecue for 8–10 minutes on each side. Meanwhile, thread the onion wedges onto 2 metal skewers, spray with oil, and barbecue for 5 minutes on each side.

Place the beets, carrots, and onion in a bowl with the arugula and pecan nuts.

Make the dressing. Blend the ingredients together in a food processor or blender until smooth and season to taste. Arrange the salad on a platter and serve drizzled with the goat cheese dressing.

For tangy mustard vinaigrette, instead of the dressing, beat together 3 tablespoons extra virgin olive oil, 1 tablespoon red wine vinegar, 2 teaspoons wholegrain mustard, a pinch of superfine sugar, and some salt and black pepper. Prepare the salad as above, and serve with the mustard vinaigrette drizzled over.

chickpea & vegetable salad

Serves **4**
Preparation time **10 minutes**
Cooking time **8 minutes**

4 **shallots**
2 **garlic cloves**, sliced
4 large **red Spanish chilies**,
   halved lengthwise and
   seeded
10 oz can **chickpeas**, rinsed
   and drained
bunch of **mint**, roughly
   chopped
3 tablespoons **olive oil**
4 tablespoons **lemon juice**
salt and **black pepper**

Heat a ridged grill pan. Cut the shallots into wedges, keeping the root ends intact to hold the wedges together, and thread them onto a metal skewer. Thread the garlic cloves onto another skewer and the chilies onto a third.

Place all the skewers on a hot barbecue and cook the garlic for 1 minute on each side, the chilies for 2–3 minutes on each side, and the shallots for 4 minutes on each side. Remove and place the vegetables in a large bowl.

Add the drained chickpeas, chopped mint, olive oil, lemon juice, and seasoning to the bowl of griddled vegetables. Mix all the ingredients together roughly and serve.

For bulghur wheat & grilled vegetable salad, cook the vegetables as above and make a double quantity of the dressing (without the chickpeas). Meanwhile, soak ¾ cup dried bulghur wheat in about 2½ cups boiling water for 20 minutes, then drain and toss with the vegetables and dressing.

smoked garlic caesar salad

Serves **4**
Preparation time **10 minutes**
Cooking time **10–12 minutes**

2 large slices of **sourdough bread**
olive oil, for brushing
4 **bacon slices**
2 **romaine lettuce hearts**, torn
12 drained **anchovy fillets**
2 **eggs**, hard-cooked, shelled and quartered

Dressing
3 **garlic cloves**
1 **egg yolk**
2 teaspoons **white wine vinegar**
4 drained **anchovy fillets**
5 tablespoons **olive oil**
3 tablespoons freshly grated **Parmesan cheese**
salt and **black pepper**

Start by making the dressing. Thread the garlic cloves onto a metal skewer and cook on a medium barbecue for 6–8 minutes until soft and lightly charred. Allow to cool. Place the garlic in a food processor or blender with the remaining ingredients and blend until smooth. Add a little boiling water to thin the sauce, if necessary.

Brush the sourdough bread with a little oil and toast for 1 minute on each side until browned. Cut into cubes and place in a large bowl. Barbecue the bacon until crisp, then allow to cool and tear into bite-size pieces. Add the lettuce leaves, anchovies, and egg quarters. Drizzle the dressing over the salad, toss well, and serve.

For grilled chicken Caesar salad, cut 2 x 8 oz chicken breast fillets in half horizontally so you have 4 thin steaks. Season well, brush with oil, and barbecue on a high heat for 4–5 minutes on each side. Cut into strips and toss with the salad above.

pepper & asparagus salad

Serves **4**

Preparation time **10 minutes**

Cooking time **10 minutes**

4 **red bell peppers**, quartered,
 cored, and seeded

7 oz **asparagus**, trimmed

2 **red chilies**

4 tablespoons **olive oil**

1 tablespoon **balsamic
 vinegar**

3 oz **Parmesan cheese**

salt and **black pepper**

Cook the pepper quarters and asparagus on a hot barbecue for 5 minutes on each side, then set aside. Meanwhile, cook the chilies, turning frequently, for a total of 3 minutes, then set aside.

Seed the red chilies and cut the flesh into very thin strips.

Arrange the vegetables on a serving plate. Drizzle with the oil and balsamic vinegar and sprinkle with salt and pepper. Peel thin ribbons of Parmesan, using a vegetable peeler, and sprinkle over the vegetables. Serve with bread toasted on the barbecue or as a side dish to accompany barbecued fish or poultry.

For pepper, asparagus, & goat cheese tortilla wraps, cook the peppers, asparagus, and chilies as above and slice the chilies. Divide the cooked vegetables between 4 flour tortillas and top each with 1 oz crumbled goat cheese and a handful of arugula leaves. Roll the tortillas up and serve.

beef salad with mustard dressing

Serves **4**
Preparation time **15 minutes**
Cooking time **8–10 minutes**

4 **beef tenderloin steaks**,
 about 7 oz each
olive oil, for brushing and
 drizzling
2 tablespoons chopped
 thyme
4 slices of **sourdough bread**
2 **garlic cloves**
1¼ cups **watercress leaves**
1¼ cups **wild arugula leaves**
2 tablespoons drained **capers**
salt and **black pepper**

Dressing
3 tablespoons **sour cream**
1 tablespoon **wholegrain
 mustard**
1 teaspoon **white wine
 vinegar**
2 tablespoons snipped **chives**
1 tablespoon boiling **water**

Brush the beef with oil and rub in the thyme, salt, and pepper. Cook on a medium barbecue for 3–4 minutes on each side. Rest in foil for 5 minutes, then slice thinly.

Meanwhile, to make the dressing, beat the sour cream, mustard, vinegar, and chives together, then gradually beat in the measured water and some salt and pepper until evenly blended.

Toast the bread slices on the barbecue for 1 minute on each side until browned. Rub with the garlic and drizzle with oil. Top each with some salad leaves, capers, and beef slices and pour the dressing over.

For chargrilled beef tenderloin with walnut pesto, place ½ cup walnuts, 3 drained cornichons, 1 crushed garlic clove, 1 tablespoon drained capers, 2 tablespoons chopped parsley, 6 tablespoons extra virgin olive oil, and some salt and pepper in a food processor or blender and blend until fairly smooth. Cook the beef steaks following the above method and serve topped with the pesto and a Tomato & Olive Salad (see page 86).

mediterranean couscous salad

Serves **4**
Preparation time **15 minutes**
Cooking time **10 minutes**

2 **red onions**
2 **garlic cloves**
2 **green chilies**
1 **eggplant**, sliced
1 **red bell pepper**
1 **zucchini**, sliced lengthwise
⅔ cup **couscous**
½ teaspoon **cumin**
½ teaspoon **paprika**
pinch of **dried red pepper
   flakes**
5 tablespoons **olive oil**
salt and **black pepper**

To garnish
bunch of **cilantro**, chopped
1 **lemon**, griddled and cut into
   wedges (optional)

Cut the red onions into wedges, keeping the root ends intact to hold the wedges together.

Thread the garlic cloves and chilies onto separate metal skewers, then cook all the vegetables on a hot barbecue as follows, removing them when charred on all sides to a large serving bowl: eggplant, pepper, and red onions for 5 minutes on each side; zucchini for 4 minutes on each side; chilies for 2–3 minutes on each side, and garlic for 1 minute on each side.

Place the couscous in a bowl and add enough hot water to cover. Leave for 5 minutes to allow all the water to be absorbed.

Peel the chilies and pepper when cool enough to handle, then seed them. Roughly chop all the vegetables and add them to the bowl of couscous. Add the cumin, paprika, pepper flakes, and seasoning, and mix well. Drizzle with the olive oil and garnish with the chopped cilantro and lemon wedges, if using.

For grilled vegetable, feta, & mint salad, prepare and cook all the vegetables as above and combine in a large bowl. Add 7 oz crumbled feta cheese, ⅔ cup pitted black olives, and a handful of torn fresh mint leaves. Beat together 3 tablespoons extra virgin olive oil, the juice of ½ lemon, 1 teaspoon honey, ½ teaspoon ground cumin, and some salt and pepper, add to the salad and stir.

prosciutto & vegetable salad

Serves **4**
Preparation time **10 minutes**
Cooking time **18 minutes**

2 **red onions**
2 **red bell peppers**, cored,
    seeded, and cut into large
    pieces
2 **zucchini**, cut into long
    lengths
1 **eggplant**, cut into long
    lengths
1 bunch of **asparagus**,
    trimmed
8 slices of **prosciutto**
bunch of **basil**, roughly
    chopped
4 tablespoons **olive oil**
2 tablespoons **balsamic
    vinegar**
salt and **black pepper**
basil sprig, to garnish

Cut the red onions into wedges, keeping the root
ends intact to hold the wedges together. Cook all the
vegetables on a hot barbecue as follows, removing
them when cooked to a large serving bowl: onions
for 5 minutes on each side; bell peppers for 5 minutes
on the skin side only; zucchini for 3 minutes on each
side; eggplant for 4 minutes on each side, and the
asparagus for 4 minutes on one side only. (If all the
vegetables are put on at the same time, you will need
to remove them in the following order: asparagus,
peppers, zucchini, eggplant, onions.) When all the
vegetables have been barbecued, toss them together
well in the bowl.

Place the slices of prosciutto on the grill rack to cook
for 4 minutes on each side, or until crispy.

Add the basil to the vegetables with the olive oil,
balsamic vinegar, and a little seasoning. Top the
vegetables with the crispy prosciutto and serve
immediately, garnished with a sprig of basil.

For beef tenderloin & vegetable salad, season a
1½ lb beef tenderloin and brush with oil. Cook on
a medium-hot barbecue for 25 minutes, turning
halfway through, then wrap in foil and allow to rest
for 10 minutes. Meanwhile, prepare and cook the
vegetables as above and add the dressing, omitting
the prosciutto. Slice the beef thickly and serve with
the grilled vegetable salad.

cypriot chicken & haloumi salad

Serves **4**
Preparation time **20 minutes**,
  plus marinating
Cooking time **20–24 minutes**

3 skinless **chicken breast**
  fillets, about 4 oz each
bunch of **oregano**, chopped
1 tablespoon **olive oil**
8 oz **haloumi cheese**
salt and **black pepper**

Cypriot salad
1 **cucumber**, skinned, seeded,
  and cut lengthwise into short
  batons
4 **beefsteak tomatoes**,
  skinned, seeded, and cut
  into wedges
1 **red onion**, finely chopped
bunch of **flat leaf parsley**,
  roughly chopped
3 tablespoons **olive oil**
1 tablespoon **wine vinegar**
salt and **black pepper**

Place the chicken in a bowl. Add the chopped oregano, olive oil, and seasoning. Allow to marinate at room temperature for 2 hours.

Cook the chicken on a hot barbecue for about 6–8 minutes on each side, then remove, cut into chunks, and keep warm.

Meanwhile, make the salad. Place the cucumber, tomato wedges, chopped red onion, and parsley in a bowl. Add the olive oil and wine vinegar, toss well and season to taste.

Slice the haloumi into 8 and griddle the slices for 4 minutes on each side then serve with the chicken and salad.

For grilled haloumi with lemon, cut 8 oz haloumi cheese into 12 slices and cook on a preheated flat plate (gas barbecue) or in a ridged griddle pan (charcoal barbecue) for 1 minute on each side until charred. Transfer to a platter and immediately squeeze over the juice of ½ lemon, drizzle with a little oil, and dress with some chopped fresh parsley. Serve at once.

lime yogurt marinade

Makes **1 cup**
Preparation time **5 minutes**,
  plus chilling

⅔ cup **plain yogurt**
2 tablespoons chopped **mint**
grated zest and juice of ½ **lime**
1 **garlic clove**, crushed
½ teaspoon **cumin**
pinch of **superfine sugar**
salt and **black pepper**

Place all the ingredients in a bowl and season to taste. Cover the bowl and chill for 1 hour for the flavors to infuse. Use as required.

For tandoori marinade, combine ⅔ cup plain yogurt with 2 crushed garlic cloves, 2 teaspoons peeled and grated fresh ginger root, 2 teaspoons ready-made tandoori spice paste, 2 teaspoons lemon juice, and a little salt and pepper. Use to marinate chicken thigh fillets and cook on a hot barbecue.

barbecue sauce with chocolate

Makes ¾ **cup**
Preparation time **5 minutes**
Cooking time **20 minutes**

2 tablespoons **olive oil**
1 small **onion**, finely chopped
1 **garlic clove**, crushed
2 teaspoons **ground coriander**
1 teaspoon **ground cumin**
½ teaspoon **ground cinnamon**
13 oz can **chopped tomatoes**
3 tablespoons **maple syrup**
3 tablespoons **red wine vinegar**
1–2 teaspoons **hot chili sauce**
½ oz **semisweet chocolate**, chopped
salt and **pepper**

Heat the oil in a saucepan and gently fry the onion, garlic, and spices for 10 minutes until soft but not browned. Add the tomatoes, maple syrup, vinegar, chili sauce, and some salt and pepper and bring to a boil. Simmer gently for 10 minutes, stir in the chocolate until melted and allow to cool.

Transfer to a food processor or blender and blend until smooth. Use as required or store in an airtight container in the refrigerator for up to 1 week.

For sweet chili barbecue sauce, combine 2 tablespoons tomato paste with 2 tablespoons sweet chili sauce and 1 tablespoon dark soy sauce. Season with a little pepper. Use to baste chicken before cooking on a hot barbecue.

moroccan spice paste

Makes ⅔ **cup**
Preparation time **5 minutes**

bunch of **cilantro**, including
  roots, roughly chopped
bunch of **parsley**, roughly
  chopped
½ cup **extra virgin olive oil**
2 **garlic cloves**, roughly
  chopped
2 teaspoons **white wine**
  vinegar
1 teaspoon **lemon juice**
1 teaspoon **ground coriander**
1 teaspoon **paprika**
1 teaspoon **ground cumin**
salt and **cayenne pepper**,
  to taste

Place the cilantro and parsley, including the stems
and roots, in a food processor or blender. Add all
of the remaining ingredients and blend to form a
smooth paste.

Use as required or store in an airtight container in
the refrigerator for up to 3 days.

For spicy herb paste, blend together 4 tablespoons
chopped herbs such as parsley, basil, mint, and
cilantro, 2 chopped garlic cloves, 1 seeded and
chopped large green chili, grated zest of 1 lemon,
½ cup extra virgin olive oil, and some salt and pepper.
Use to marinate chicken or fish fillets.

rosemary, coriander, & lemon rub

Makes **5 tablespoons**
Cooking time **2–3 minutes**
Preparation time **5 minutes**

2 tablespoons **coriander
seeds**
2 tablespoons chopped
rosemary
grated zest of 1 **lemon**
salt and **black pepper**

Dry-fry the coriander seeds in a skillet over a high heat for 2–3 minutes until they begin to pop and release their aroma. Cool the spices and mix with the rosemary, lemon zest, and some salt and pepper.

Use as required or store in an airtight container for up to 2 weeks.

For fennel rub, dry-fry 2 tablespoons fennel seeds and 1 tablespoon black peppercorns in a small skillet over a medium heat for 1–2 minutes until they begin to brown and release their aroma. Allow to cool then grind in a spice grinder until fairly fine. Transfer to a bowl and stir in ¼ teaspoon salt. Use as required.

smoky barbecue rub

Makes **5 tablespoons**
Preparation time **5 minutes**

1 tablespoon **salt**
1 tablespoon **smoked paprika**
1 teaspoon **ground coriander**
2 teaspoons crushed **black pepper**
2 teaspoons **powdered mustard**
1 teaspoon **superfine sugar**
¼ teaspoon **cayenne pepper**

Combine the ingredients in a bowl and stir well. Transfer to an airtight container or use as required. This will keep fresh for up to 2 weeks.

For Asian-style barbecue rub, grind together 4 whole star anise, 2 teaspoons Szechuan peppercorns, 1 teaspoon fennel seeds, 1 cinnamon stick, and 6 whole cloves. Mix with 2 crushed garlic cloves, the grated zest of 2 limes, and 1 teaspoon salt. Store as above or use as required.

smoked garlic oil

Makes ½ **cup**
Preparation time **10 minutes**,
   plus soaking
Cooking time **30 minutes**

1 **garlic bulb**, unpeeled
8 oz **hickory chips**
½ cup **extra virgin olive oil**
salt and **black pepper**

Place the garlic bulb in a bowl with the wood chips and cover well with cold water. Allow to soak for 30 minutes, then drain.

Lay a double layer of foil about 12 inches square on the work surface and place the wood chips in the center in a shallow pile. Fold the foil over the chips and seal the edges to form a pillow-shaped parcel. Using a knife, stab a dozen small holes in the top.

Heat the barbecue to medium and, using the indirect cooking method (see page 12), place the foil parcel over the unlit gas burner (or in the center of the coal barbecue) and place the garlic on the rack in the roasting pan. Cover and cook for 30 minutes.

Remove the garlic, wrap loosely in foil, and allow to cool completely. Trim the top of the garlic and squeeze the paste into a mortar and pestle and pound to a paste. Transfer to a jar and add the oil and some salt and pepper. Use as required or store in an airtight container in the refrigerator for up to 3 days.

For rosemary oil, place 2 rosemary sprigs in a clean, dry bottle and top up with extra virgin olive oil, making sure the tops of the rosemary sprigs are covered. Place in a cool dark place for 3–4 days, then drain the oil into a clean jar. Use as required.

citrus, chili, & fresh thyme oil

Makes 2½ **cups**
Preparation time **5 minutes**,
  plus infusing

peel of 1 **lemon**, cut into long,
  thin strips
peel of 1 **lime**, cut into long,
  thin strips
1 large **red chili**, seeded and
  sliced
6 **thyme sprigs**, bruised
1 teaspoon **black**
  peppercorns, lightly crushed
2½ cups **extra virgin olive oil**
salt

Place the lemon and lime peel in a bowl and add the chili, thyme sprigs, peppercorns, and a little salt. Pour in the oil, cover, and allow to infuse in a cool, dark place for 3–4 days.

Strain the oil through a fine sieve into a bottle and use as required.

For piri-piri, a fiery chili oil, pour 2½ cups extra virgin olive oil into a bottle and add 2 tablespoons dried red pepper flakes and a pinch of salt. Allow to infuse for 3 days, then use as required, leaving the pepper flakes in the oil.

sweet treats

mango with strawberry ice

Serves **6**
Preparation time **10 minutes**,
  plus freezing
Cooking time **6 minutes**

½ cup **granulated sugar**
1¼ cups **water**
grated zest and juice of
  1 lemon
5 tablespoons **white rum**
3 cups **strawberries**, hulled
3 large ripe **mangoes**
2 tablespoons **light brown
  sugar**
½ teaspoon **Chinese
  five-spice powder**

Put the granulated sugar, water, lemon zest and juice into a saucepan and heat gently until the sugar is dissolved, then boil for 3 minutes. Remove from the heat and stir in the rum, then allow to cool.

Place the strawberries in a food processor or blender with the cooled syrup and blend until completely smooth. Transfer to a plastic container and freeze. Beat the mixture after 1 hour, then beat again every 30 minutes until you have a soft sorbet texture. Alternatively, churn in an ice cream maker until slushy. Freeze until required.

Cut the mangoes down each side of the pit and then cut each piece in half. Combine the brown sugar and spice powder and dust lightly over the mango portions. Cook on a medium barbecue for 2–3 minutes on each side until charred. Serve with the strawberry ice.

For quick butterscotch sauce, which you could serve with the barbecued mango, mix ¾ cup Greek or whole milk yogurt with 4 tablespoons light brown sugar and ½ teaspoon vanilla essence.

honeyed strawberry mousses

Serves **6**

Preparation time **30 minutes**, plus freezing

Cooking time **2 minutes**

3 tablespoons **water**

3 teaspoons **powdered gelatin** or 1 envelope

2⅔ cups **strawberries**, hulled, plus extra, halved, to decorate (optional)

6 teaspoons **set honey**

1¼ cups **fat-free plain yogurt**

2 **passion fruit**, halved

Put the water in a small cup and sprinkle with the gelatin, making sure that all the powder absorbs water. Set aside for 5 minutes to soak.

Puree half the strawberries with 2 teaspoons of the honey in a food processor or blender until smooth, then pour into a pitcher.

Stand the cup of gelatin in a small saucepan of simmering water and heat until it dissolves and the liquid is clear.

Stir 3 teaspoons of gelatin into the strawberry puree and divide between 6 individual ⅔ cup metal pudding molds. Freeze for 15 minutes until just set.

Puree the remaining strawberries with the remaining honey. Add the yogurt and blend together. Gradually mix in the remaining gelatin and pour over the set strawberry layer in the pudding molds. Freeze for 4–5 hours until set.

Dip each mold into just-boiled water, count to 5, loosen the edges with a fingertip, then invert each one onto a plate. Holding plate and mold together, jerk to release the mousse. Spoon passion fruit seeds around the desserts and decorate with halved strawberries, if desired.

For strawberry skewers with chocolate dipping sauce, make some chocolate sauce (see page 208). Meanwhile, thread 20 large strawberries onto soaked bamboo skewers, sprinkle with confectioners' sugar and cook on a hot barbecue for 2 minutes until starting to sizzle and ooze. Serve with chocolate sauce.

soufflé omelet with strawberries

Serves **4**
Preparation time **15 minutes**
Cooking time **8–10 minutes**

2¼ cups **strawberries**, hulled
and thickly sliced, plus extra
to decorate
2 tablespoons **red currant
jelly**
2 teaspoons **balsamic
vinegar**
5 **eggs**, separated
4 tablespoons **confectioners'
sugar**, sifted
2 tablespoons **butter**

Warm the sliced strawberries, red currant jelly, and vinegar together in a saucepan until the jelly has just melted.

Meanwhile, beat the egg whites into stiff, moist-looking peaks. Mix the egg yolks with 1 tablespoon of the sugar, then fold into the egg whites.

Heat the butter in a large skillet, add the egg mixture and cook over a medium heat for 3–4 minutes until the underside is golden. Quickly transfer the pan to a hot broiler and cook for 2–3 minutes until the top is browned and the center still slightly soft, making sure that the handle is away from the heat.

Spoon the warm strawberry mixture over the omelet, fold in half, and dust with the remaining sugar. Cut into 4 and serve immediately with extra strawberries.

For sweet soufflé omelet with cherries & cinnamon ice cream, make the omelet following the recipe above. Strain ¾ cup canned or bottled pitted morello cherries and serve with the omelet and a spoonful of cinnamon ice cream.

chocolate & banana melt

Serves **4**

Preparation time **5 minutes**

Cooking time **2–4 minutes**

8 slices of **white bread**, crusts
removed

3 oz **semisweet chocolate**,
finely chopped

1 large **banana**, sliced

1 cup **marshmallows**,
chopped

spray oil

Place half the bread slices on the work surface and top each with chocolate, banana, and marshmallows. Top with the remaining bread.

Spray the sandwiches with oil and cook on the flat plate of a gas barbecue or on a rack over charcoal for 1–2 minutes. Spray the top side with a little oil, flip and cook for an additional 1–2 minutes until golden. Serve with vanilla ice cream, if desired.

For toasted marshmallows with chocolate dipping sauce, combine ⅔ cup light cream, 5 oz chopped semisweet chocolate and 1 tablespoon butter in a bowl set over a saucepan of gently simmering water (do not let the bowl touch the water). Stir frequently until the chocolate has melted and the mixture is smooth. Remove from the heat and cool slightly. Spear marshmallows onto metal skewers and cook over a hot barbecue (make sure the marshmallows don't actually touch the grill or you'll have a sticky mess). Serve with the chocolate sauce.

hot barbecued fruit salad

Serves **4**

Preparation time **15 minutes**

Cooking time **8 minutes**

1 small **pineapple**

1 **mango**

1 **nectarine**, quartered and
  pitted

1 **peach**, quartered and pitted

2 **apricots**, halved, or
  quartered if large, and pitted

4 tablespoons **Greek** or
  whole milk yogurt

honey, for drizzling

few **cardamom seeds**
  (optional)

Top and tail the pineapple and place it on one end on
a cutting board. Using a sharp knife, cut downwards to
remove the skin, working all around the pineapple. Cut
the pineapple flesh into chunks—in a small pineapple
the core is usually sweet and soft enough to eat.

Peel the mango and cut it into slices on either side
of the pit. Cook the mango and pineapple on a hot
barbecue for 4 minutes on each side and the nectarine,
peach, and apricots for 3 minutes on each side. If you
wish, thread the fruit pieces onto metal skewers
before cooking.

Arrange the griddled fruit in individual serving dishes.
Top each with a tablespoonful of yogurt, drizzle honey
over the top, and sprinkle with cardamom seeds, if
using, or top with spoonfuls of Caramel & Cinnamon
Yogurt (see below).

For caramel & cinnamon yogurt, to serve as an
accompaniment, combine ¾ cup Greek or whole milk
yogurt in a bowl with 1 tablespoon dark brown sugar
and 1 teaspoon ground cinnamon.

lemon & honey ice

Serves **4–6**
Preparation time **20–25
  minutes**, plus cooling and
  freezing
Cooking time **2 minutes**

4 large or 6 medium **lemons**
about 4 tablespoons **water**
2 tablespoons **honey**
¼ cup **superfine sugar**
1 **bay leaf** or **lemon balm
  sprig**
2 cups **plain yogurt** or
  fromage frais
strips of **lemon zest**,
  to decorate

Slice off the top of each lemon. Carefully scoop out all the pulp and juice with a teaspoon. Discard any white pith, skin, and seeds, then puree the pulp and juice in a food processor or blender. You will need ⅔ cup. If there is less than this, top it up with water.

Put the measured water, honey, sugar, and bay leaf into a saucepan. Stir over a low heat until the sugar has dissolved, then allow to cool. Blend the mixture with the lemon puree and the yogurt. Do not remove the herb at this stage.

Pour into a freezer tray or shallow dish and freeze until lightly frozen, then gently fork the mixture and remove the herb. Return the ice to the freezer.

Transfer the ice to the refrigerator about 20 minutes before serving. Serve in individual bowls, decorated with strips of lemon zest.

For strawberry yogurt ice cream, wash and dry 3 cups strawberries, place in a blender or food processor with 2 tablespoons honey, 1 teaspoon lemon juice, and a few drops of vanilla extract and puree until smooth. Beat in 2½ cups Greek or whole milk yogurt and freeze for 6 hours, beating every hour until frozen.

barbecued bananas & ice cream

Serves **4**
Preparation time **5 minutes**,
  plus infusing and freezing
Cooking time **10 minutes**

4 large **bananas**

Ice cream
2 cups **milk**
1 cup **heavy cream**
2 **star anise**, lightly bashed
5 **egg yolks**
½ cup **maple syrup**

Start by making the ice cream. Put the milk, cream, and star anise into a saucepan and heat until boiling point is reached. Then remove from the heat and infuse for 20 minutes.

Meanwhile, beat the egg yolks and syrup together, then strain in the infused milk and return to the pan. Heat gently, stirring until the custard thickens to coat the back of a wooden spoon. Do not boil. Leave the custard until cold and then freeze in an ice cream maker, according to the manufacturer's instructions.

Place the whole bananas in their skins on the barbecue and cook for 4–5 minutes, turning halfway through until the skins are blackened. Peel and serve the banana with a scoop of ice cream.

For barbecued chocolate bananas, follow the recipe above to cook the bananas, cutting the skins open after 3 minutes. Place 2 squares of dark, milk, or white chocolate into the banana flesh and cook for the final 1–2 minutes until the chocolate is melted.

raspberry cheesecake

Serves **6–8**
Preparation time **20 minutes**,
  plus chilling
Cooking time **5 minutes**

¼ cup **butter**, melted
1½ cups crushed **Graham crackers**
3 tablespoons **orange juice**
3 teaspoons **powdered gelatin** or 1 envelope
1½ cups **low-fat cream cheese**
¼ cup **superfine sugar**
3 **eggs**, separated
1¼ cups **heavy cream**

To decorate
4 tablespoons **heavy cream**, whipped
2 cups **raspberries**

Mix the melted butter into the cracker crumbs and press the mixture into the base of a lightly oiled 8 inch springform cake pan; chill for 20 minutes until firm.

Put the orange juice in a small saucepan, sprinkle with the gelatin and allow to soak for 5 minutes. Heat gently until the gelatin dissolves and the liquid is clear.

Meanwhile, beat the cheese and sugar together in a bowl until smooth then beat in the egg yolks. Stir 2 tablespoons into the gelatin mixture and then stir this back into the main mixture.

Whip the cream until firm and fold into the cheese mixture. In a clean bowl, beat the egg whites until stiff, stir 2 tablespoons into the cheese mixture to lighten it. Fold in the remaining egg whites until evenly combined.

Spoon the mixture over the cracker base and level the surface. Chill for 1–1½ hours or until the filling is set. Pipe a whipped cream border around the edge of the cheesecake and arrange the raspberries over the top. Cut into wedges to serve.

For lemon, ginger, & blueberry cheesecake, make the cracker crust using 1½ cups crushed gingersnaps, replace the orange juice with lemon juice, and add 2 teaspoons grated lemon zest to the cream cheese, sugar, and egg yolks. Serve the cheesecake in wedges with whipped cream and fresh blueberries.

grilled pineapple with granita

Serves **6**

Preparation time **10 minutes**,
  plus freezing

Cooking time **12–14 minutes**

1 **pineapple**, 1½ lb

⅓ cup **palm sugar** or **dark
  brown sugar**

Lime & **mint granita**

1 cup **granulated sugar**

2 cups cold **water**

4 strips of **lime peel**

4 large **mint sprigs**, bruised

1 cup **lime juice** (from about
  6 large limes)

3 tablespoons **vodka**

Make the granita. Place the sugar, measured water, and lime peel in a saucepan, heat gently to dissolve the sugar and then bring to a boil. Simmer for 5 minutes, remove from the heat, and stir in the mint. Allow to cool and then strain.

Stir the lime juice and vodka into the sugar syrup and transfer to a bowl. Place in the freezer for about 4 hours until frozen.

Remove the ice from the freezer for 15 minutes to soften then transfer to a food processor and blend for 30 seconds until soft and pale. Freeze again if necessary.

Top and tail the pineapple and place it on one end on a cutting board. Using a sharp knife, cut downwards to remove the skin, working all around the pineapple. Quarter and core the pineapple, then cut the flesh into wedges. Spike onto 6 metal skewers, dip in the sugar, and barbecue over a medium heat for 2–3 minutes on each side until golden. Cool slightly and serve with the granita.

For grilled pineapple popsicles, prepare the pineapple as above but cut the wedges into chunks. Skewer the chunks onto presoaked bamboo skewers, dust with a little palm or brown sugar and cook as above. Serve the popsicles with some plain yogurt flavored with honey and a squeeze of fresh lemon juice.

strawberry kebabs with ice cream

Serves **4**
Preparation time **5 minutes**
Cooking time **3–4 minutes**

3 cups **strawberries**, washed
    but unhulled
2 cup carton luxury **ice cream**
    (such as vanilla, strawberry,
    or chocolate)

Soak 8 bamboo skewers in cold water for 30 minutes. Thread the strawberries onto the skewers and cook on a hot barbecue for 3–4 minutes, turning frequently.

Meanwhile, spoon scoops of luxury ice cream into 4 serving dishes. Spoon the griddled strawberries on top and serve.

For grilled figs with ice cream, cut 8 large, just-ripe figs in half and dust lightly with confectioners' sugar. Cook on a hot barbecue for 2–3 minutes, tuning halfway through until tender, then serve with hazelnut or cinnamon ice cream.

lemon & honeycomb stacks

Serves **2**
Preparation time **6 minutes**
Cooking time **2–4 minutes**

4 tablespoons **heavy cream**,
plus extra to serve
1½ oz **honeycomb** or **old-
fashioned cinder taffy**,
crumbled
1 teaspoon finely grated
lemon zest
⅛ cup finely chopped **candied
lemon peel** (optional)
⅔ cup traditional **lemon curd**
6 **pancakes**
blueberries, to serve

Put the cream, honeycomb, lemon zest, candied peel, if using, and lemon curd in a bowl and mix well. Place a dollop of the lemon cream on a pancake, top with a second pancake and another dollop of lemon cream on top, then finish with a third pancake. Repeat the process so that you have two triple-decker lemon pancakes.

Cook the pancake stacks on a medium-hot barbecue for 1–2 minutes, then flip over and cook for the same time until the outside pancakes are toasted and the lemon cream is beginning to ooze from the sides. Serve immediately with some blueberries.

For sweet bruschetta with lemon cream & honeycomb, make the lemon cream as above. Toast 2 slices of brioche or raisin bread lightly on the barbecue, top with a spoonful of the lemon cream and serve topped with mixed fresh berries dusted with confectioners' sugar.

fruit parcels with caramel sauce

Serves **4**
Preparation time **10 minutes**
Cooking time **15 minutes**

6 **figs**, quartered
2 **peaches**, pitted and
  quartered
1½ cups **blueberries**

Caramel sauce
¼ cup **unsalted butter**
¾ cup **light brown sugar**
2 tablespoons **corn syrup**
5 tablespoons **heavy cream**
few drops of **vanilla extract**

Make the sauce. Melt the butter in a small saucepan over a medium heat, add the sugar and syrup and cook gently until the sugar dissolves. Stir in the cream and vanilla extract and bring slowly to boiling point. Remove from the heat and allow to stand while cooking the foil parcels.

Lay 4 pieces of foil on the work surface and arrange a pile of the fruit in the middle of each one. Seal the parcels, then cook on a low heat on the barbecue for 8–10 minutes. Carefully open the parcels and serve the fruit topped with the caramel sauce.

For grilled figs with Amaretto cream, cut 6 just-ripe figs in half and sprinkle the cut sides with a little brown sugar. Cook cut-side up on a medium heat for 3–4 minutes until the figs are tender. Meanwhile, lightly whip ⅔ cup heavy cream with 1 tablespoon confectioners' sugar and 1 tablespoon Amaretto liqueur until just firm. Serve with the figs.

fruit salad cups

Serves **6**
Preparation time **45 minutes**
Cooking time **15 minutes**

1 large **mango**
1¼ cups **raspberries**
1 cup **blueberries**
¾ cup **plain yogurt**
sifted **confectioners' sugar**,
  to decorate

Tuile cups
2 **egg whites**
¼ cup **superfine sugar**
3 tablespoons **sunflower oil**
few drops of **vanilla extract**
6 tablespoons **all-purpose
  flour**

Line 3 baking sheets with nonstick parchment paper. Put the egg whites in a bowl and fork together until frothy but still clear. Add the sugar, oil, and vanilla extract and mix together.

Sift the flour into the bowl and stir together. Spoon the mixture into 6 mounds on the baking sheets and spread each to a circle, about 5 inches across.

Place one of the baking sheets in a preheated oven, 375°F, for about 5 minutes until the cookies are light brown in the center and slightly darker around the edges. Remove from the oven and allow to stand for 30 seconds. Put a second sheet in the oven, then repeat with the third.

Loosen the cooked cookies. Working quickly, drape each cookie over a large orange and pinch the edges to make a fluted edge. Allow to set for a few minutes then lift off the oranges, turn up the other way and put onto a cooling rack. Repeat to make 6 cups.

Stand the mango on its side and cut a thick slice off each side. Cut the flesh away from the pit and peel and cut the flesh into slices. Mix with the berries. Spoon the yogurt, then the fruit into the cups. Transfer to serving plates, dust with confectioners' sugar, and serve immediately with passion fruit sauce (see below).

For passion fruit sauce, heat together in a saucepan ½ cup superfine sugar and ½ cup water, stirring over a low heat until the sugar dissolves. Add ⅓ cup passion fruit pulp (from about 6 fruits), bring to a boil and simmer for 10 minutes until it forms a sauce. Allow to cool and serve at room temperature.

raspberry & mascarpone brioche

Serves **4**
Preparation time **5 minutes**
Cooking time **1–2 minutes**

4 slices of **brioche** or
   raisin bread
2 cups **raspberries**

Vanilla mascarpone
1 cup **mascarpone cheese**
2 tablespoons **light cream**
seeds from 1 **vanilla bean**
1–2 tablespoons
   confectioners' sugar,
   plus extra to dust

Make the vanilla mascarpone. Stir the mascarpone, cream, vanilla seeds, and confectioners' sugar together until smooth—do not overbeat.

Toast the brioche slices on a medium barbecue for 30 seconds on each side until lightly browned. Top with the raspberries and vanilla mascarpone and dust with confectioners' sugar.

For brioche with blistered peaches, cut 6 peaches in half and remove the pits. Dust with a little confectioners' sugar and barbecue on a medium heat for 1–2 minutes on each side until charred and tender. Combine 1 cup mascarpone cheese with 2 tablespoons light cream, 1 teaspoon almond extract, and a pinch of ground mixed spice. Serve with the peaches.

summer berry roulade

Serves **8**
Preparation time **30 minutes**
Cooking time **20 minutes**

4 eggs
½ cup **superfine sugar**, plus
   extra for sprinkling
grated zest of **1 lemon**
1 cup **all-purpose flour**

Filling
1 cup **plain yogurt**
½ cup **ricotta cheese**
1 tablespoon **superfine sugar**
1 cup **blueberries**
1¼ cups **raspberries**

Line the base and sides of a 12 x 9 inch jelly roll pan with a single sheet of nonstick parchment paper, cutting the paper in the corners. Put the eggs, sugar, and lemon zest in a mixing bowl set over a saucepan of simmering water. With an electric beater, beat the mixture for 10 minutes until it is thick and the mixture leaves a trail over the surface when the beaters are raised.

Remove the bowl from the saucepan, sift the flour over the surface and gently fold in. Pour the mixture into the pan. Bake in a preheated oven, 400°F, for 8–10 minutes until the top springs back when pressed with a fingertip.

Put a piece of nonstick parchment paper (about the same size as the pan) on the work surface with a narrow edge toward you and sprinkle with sugar. Quickly turn the sponge cake out onto the paper, peel off the lining paper and cover with a second piece of paper. Loosely roll up the cake, starting from the edge nearest you. Leave loosely wrapped in the sugared paper to cool.

Unroll the cake and remove the center paper. Mix the yogurt and ricotta with the sugar and spread over the cake. Sprinkle with the fruit, reserving a few for decoration, then re-roll the cake, using the sugared paper underneath to help you (but being careful not to roll the paper up inside the roulade) and transfer to a serving plate. Decorate with the remaining fruit and serve cut into thick slices.

bananas, fruit sauce, & ice cream

Serves **4**
Preparation time **10 minutes**
Cooking time **25 minutes**

1 ¼ cups **dried peaches** or **apricots**
¾ cup **pineapple juice**
1 teaspoon **ground cinnamon**
4 **bananas**
vanilla ice cream

Place the peaches or apricots, pineapple juice, and cinnamon in a saucepan and bring to a boil. Reduce the heat and simmer for 10 minutes, or until the fruits are soft. Cool slightly, then place in a food processor or blender and process until smooth.

Cook the whole bananas in their skins on a hot barbecue for 4–5 minutes, turning halfway through, until the skins are blackened.

Peel the bananas. Serve each with scoops of vanilla ice cream and spoonfuls of the sauce.

For maple & pecan fudge sauce, an alternative sauce to serve with the grilled bananas, heat ⅓ cup unsalted butter, ⅓ cup maple syrup, and ⅓ cup heavy cream together in a small pan set on a low heat until the butter melts. Simmer for 5 minutes until thickened, then stir in ¾ cup pecan nuts. Simmer for another minute, then allow to cool. Serve warm.

index

acknowledgments

Executive Editor: Nicky Hill
Editor: Amy Corbett
Executive Art Editor: Mark Stevens
Designer: Rebecca Johns for Cobalt id
Photographer: Ian Wallace
Food Stylist: Louise Pickford
Production Controller: Carolin Stransky

Commissioned photography © Octopus Publishing
Group Ltd/Ian Wallace apart from the following:
© Octopus Publishing Group Limited/Graham Kirk 35;
Gus Filgate 51, 127, 141; Ian Wallace 109, 119, 147,
213; Lis Parsons 207, 223; Peter Myers 95, 101, 131,
217; Sean Myers 103, 165, 169, 173, 177, 181, 183,
185, 211, 221, 233; Stephen Conroy 81, 85; William
Lingwood 69, 205, 227, 231; William Reavell 23.